VITAL

CHURCHES CHANGING COMMUNITIES AND THE WORLD

Jorge Acevedo has been doing ministry this way for a long time. He is better than anyone I know of contextualizing the genius of Wesley's balance of head, heart and hands in personal and social holiness for our day. He is clear about the being intentional to lead people to Jesus AND meet their needs--and the result is a people who are in the process of becoming wholly holy. Persons are accepted exactly where they are in the midst of life's broken places, AND are given the places and spaces to be made whole as their lives are being transformed as they follow after Jesus.

Long before Jorge was preaching on Conference platforms, he was leading the people of his congregation to pray and ask God to send them people that nobody else wants or sees--and the result has been astonishing. Drawing people from Main Street and the margins, Grace Church has grown from one campus to four--and from 300 to nearly 3,000.

I have been Jorge's friend and colleague for thirty years--and this book captures the essence of why he is such as effective leader and his church is so VITAL."

–**Jeff Greenway**, Lead Pastor, Reynoldsburg UMC

"If the Call to Action is an instrument of renewal for our church—and I believe it can be—it will happen one local church and one annual conference at a time. Jorge Acevedo's influence is grounded in a local church that makes disciples of Jesus Christ for the transformation of the world in profound and provocative ways. I am grateful for God for the witness in these pages and the lives that have been and will be changed by the power of the lived experience of Christianity in our Wesleyan tradition."

–**Ken Carter**, Resident Bishop, Florida Area, United Methodist Church

Nobody weds Wesley's doctrine of personal piety and social holiness together like Jorge does. In this book he describes in a straight forward way how he assembled a team that grew their church from 300 to close to 3000. By searching for the people nobody sees or wants they have created the only blue color (or no collar!) mega church in Methodism. Jorge is a light well worth following."

–**Phillip Connolly**, active UM layman,
General Conference delegate, West Ohio Conference

If you are going to read one book this year on being a more effective leader or church, this is that book. Jorge Acevedo is an outstanding leader. Vital offers the keys to effective leadership and developing highly vital congregations. Resurrection's leadership team will be studying Vital together this year.

–**Adam Hamilton**, Senior Pastor,
The United Methodist Church of the Resurrection

Jorge Acevedo is a leader who understands that the vitality of any congregation is based on the health of its pastors, staff, members, and the systems that lead to dynamic ministry. He has spent years pursuing that health in his own life and the churches he serves. By combining objective research on thousands of churches with his personal experience, he shares crucial behaviors for leaders and congregations that lead to fruitful ministry. A book that makes me take a fresh look at my ministry and leadership.

–**Tom Berlin**, Sr. Pastor, Floris UMC,
co-author of *Bearing Fruit: Ministry with Real Results*

Jorge Acevedo is no ordinary pastor. He faced challenges common to thousands of struggling churches and found ways to overcome them to change lives and communities. His words offer hope and direction. He shows what can be done through hard work, prayer, perseverance, and a vision open to continuous learning.

–**Lovett H. Weems**, Jr., distinguished professor of church leadership
and director, Lewis Center for Church Leadership, Washington, DC

Jorge and I have shared life together for over 20 years in a small covenant group of pastors. He is the "real deal." Jorge is able to write about vital churches because he enjoys an authentically vital life in Christ. Jorge clearly communicates how to experience life and vitality in your local church. This book will challenge, encourage and equip you to take your ministry to the next level of effectiveness. Jorge's book offers both a gentle hand of guidance and a swift kick in the rear to all of us in ministry! If you apply the principles in this book, you and your church will never be the same again.

–**Matthew Hartsfield**
Senior Pastor, Van Dyke Church, Tampa, FL

Jorge tells the story of a church that found its vitality in reaching the needs of people in their communities. This is the story of a traditional United Methodist Church that has exploded in its outreach by falling in love with neighbors whom Jesus loves.

The United Methodist Church in the US needs this story of hope and the lessons of faithful leadership. Jorge Acevedo tells the story of the miracle God. His story illustrates beautifully the research of what makes for a vital local church.

There are many critics of accountability for measuring vitality. We need more illustrations of how a real pastor encounters a church in real trouble and finds the real power of the Holy Spirit. Thank you, Jorge Acevedo, for being an accountable leader who also mentors lay and clergy leaders.

–**Deborah A. McLeod**, Sr. Pastor,
Mandarin United Methodist Church, Jacksonville, FL

The Wesleyan flame in Jorge's heart, his pastoral experience, and his passionate desire to see the local church be all that God intends it to be burn like an unquenchable fire in the story he tells and the practical lessons he shares. I expect this book to make a vital contribution to the renewal of the church in our time.

–**James A. Harnish**, Hyde Park United Methodist Church, Tampa, FL

Churches Changing Communities and the World

Jorge Acevedo

foreword by John Schol

Abingdon Press

Nashville

VITAL:
CHURCHES CHANGING COMMUNITIES AND THE WORLD
Copyright © 2012 by Abingdon Press.

All rights reserved.
No part of this work may be reproduced or transmitted in any form or by any means, electronic or mechanical, including photocopying and recording, or by any information storage or retrieval system, except as may be expressly permitted by the 1976 Copyright Act or in writing from the publisher. Requests for permission can be addressed to Permissions, The United Methodist Publishing House, P.O. Box 801, 201 Eighth Avenue South, Nashville, TN 37202-0801, or e-mailed to permissions@umpublishing.org.

This book is printed on acid-free paper.

Library of Congress Cataloging-in-Publication Data

ISBN 978-1-4267-6755-5

Scripture quotations unless noted otherwise are from the Common English Bible. Copyright © 2011 by the Common English Bible. All rights reserved. Used by permission. www.CommonEnglishBible.com.

Scripture quotations marked NLT are taken from the Holy Bible, New Living Translation, copyright © 1996, 2004, 2007. Used by permission of Tyndale House Publishers, Inc., Carol Stream, Illinois 60188. All rights reserved.

Scripture quotations marked (CEV) are from the Contemporary English Version Copyright © 1991, 1992, 1995 by American Bible Society, Used by Permission.

Scripture quotations from THE MESSAGE. Copyright © by Eugene H. Peterson 1993, 1994, 1995, 1996, 2000, 2001, 2002. Used by permission of NavPress Publishing Group.

Scripture quotations marked NRSV are taken from the New Revised Standard Version of the Bible, copyright 1989, Division of Christian Education of the National Council of the Churches of Christ in the United States of America. Used by permission. All rights reserved.

Scripture quotations marked (NIV) are taken from the Holy Bible, New International Version®, NIV®. Copyright © 1973, 1978, 1984, 2011 by Biblica, Inc.TM Used by permission of Zondervan. All rights reserved worldwide. www.zondervan.com. The "NIV" and "New International Version" are trademarks registered in the United States Patent and Trademark Office by Biblica, Inc.TM

Quotation from Should We Change Our Game Plan? by George Hunter (Abingdon Press, prepublication) is used by permission of the author.

12 13 14 15 16 17 18 19 20—10 9 8 7 6 5 4 3 2 1

MANUFACTURED IN THE UNITED STATES OF AMERICA

*We were glad to share not only God's good news with you
but also our very lives because we cared for you so much.*
1 Thessalonians 2:8

To three remarkable pastoral mentors who each shared themselves
and invested uniquely in my life and awakened in me the joyful
and demanding call to be a spiritual leader.

J. Howard Olds

Barbara Williams Riddle

Dick Wills

Contents

Foreword
John Schol

Life and vitality in the church are elusive and hard to get our hands around. Is it activity? Is it measures of fruitfulness? Or is it life-full stories emerging from the church? The answer is, YES! Like our lives, our vitality is a combination of a series of measures, our level of activity, and stories of life-full living.

I will never forget the puzzled look on the doctor's face when my wife, Beverly, gave birth to our second child, Kristin. After delivering and holding Kristin in his hands, the doctor looked at Kristin and looked at Beverly and looked at Kristin again and looked back at Beverly said, "This baby is too small, there must be another one. You're having twins!"

At that moment, everything in the birthing room changed. There were three nurses present. To the first nurse the doctor said, "Run and get a pediatrician;" to the second he said, "Run and get an incubator;" and to the third nurse while pointing to the monitors he said, "Watch the vital signs, watch the vital signs." I did not need a medical degree to understand his concern. We were all relieved when nine and a half minutes later Rebecca was born, healthy and full of vitality. But I will never forget those words, "Watch the vital signs."

Jorge Acevedo shares a compelling story of how the church can become more vital. He is not describing institutional survival but what Jesus described to his followers, Kingdom life.

Today we want more highly vital congregations because they change lives and demonstrate Kingdom life. Vital congregations make and mature disciples, grow over time, and engage disciples in community and world ministry that is transforming lives and addressing social issues. Vital congregations are practicing the Wesleyan means of grace and are becoming the grace of Jesus Christ in the world.

Jorge Acevedo writes about what he knows and what he has led—congregations that are vital and engaged. Congregations that have vital signs engage daily with:

Life-full stories that are being told about and through the congregation. Stories about how people's lives are transformed and stories of transforming ministries done by the congregation.

Measures of fruitfulness evident by new disciples being made, number of disciples in small groups for learning and faith formation, number of disciples engaged in worship and mission, and generous giving by disciples to mission.

The ministry activities for building up the community of faith and to transform lives and social conditions in the community and the world.

A congregation may demonstrate health with any one or two of the vital signs, but it is the combination of all three that are evidences of high vitality and Kingdom life.

Effective leaders in these congregations watch the vital signs and build on the vitality of the congregation; they encourage people to claim their story and tell the story of God's activity in and through the congregation; and these leaders know their measures of vitality and lead toward greater fruitfulness. Vital leaders lead the congregation to organize ministry to grow disciples, serve the community, and grow the congregation.

Vital Congregations focus ministry in five strategic ministry areas of vitality:

Pastoral Leadership—Pastors use their influence to help congregations set and achieve significant goals, inspire the congregation through preaching, serve in an appointment effectively and for a longer period of time, and coach and mentor laity to lead effectively.

Lay Leadership—Laity demonstrate a vital and active personal faith, develop and grow in their leadership effectiveness, and rotate new people into leadership positions so that more people have the opportunity to serve.

Worship—Vital churches offer a mix of worship services appropriate to their context, tend to use topical sermon series; for mid- to large-size congregations, they use contemporary music in contemporary worship and use multimedia in contemporary worship.

Ministry—Vital congregations offer effective and abundant opportunities for children and youth ministry and small groups.

Mission—Churches striving for vitality strategically put in place outreach programs making an impact both locally and globally.

Jorge Acevedo thoughtfully and inspirationally tells how congregations can grow their vitality based on his experience of leading vital congregations so that congregations become God's grace in the community and the world. Watch the vital signs!

Introduction

I am the vine; you are the branches. If you remain in me
and I in you, then you will produce much fruit.
Without me, you can't do anything.
John 15:5

I want to begin with a confession. I love the church! This may not sound profound upon an initial hearing, but let me give you some of my history because for me to say "I love the church" is quite radical if you know my story.

I had what you might call a nominal religious upbringing. Church was a very small part of my childhood, but I quit going to church when I was thirteen. The pastor yelled at me and my friend Alex for fooling around in the back of church during a service. I was so embarrassed that I left church that night and never returned to any church for five years. During those five years, my life spiraled into a world of drugs and alcohol. By the grace of God, a Campus Crusade for Christ area director led me to Christ shortly before I graduated from high school.

After attending a Campus Crusade for Christ summer conference in Colorado, I learned that Christ-followers were supposed to belong to local churches where they could worship, serve, give, and grow as a disciple. So in the summer of 1978, I began attending a local United Methodist church that was in the midst of tremendous growth. This was at the height of the charismatic renewal movement.

In that church, I began to grow as a Christian. In that church, I began to sense the stirrings of the Spirit calling me into pastoral ministry. In that church, my calling was affirmed and confirmed, and from that church I was sent to Asbury College and Asbury Seminary to prepare myself for a lifetime of local church ministry as a United Methodist pastor.

Upon graduation and ordination, I began ministry in the local church. And little did I know it but an underlying bias was soon to confront me. Now please hear me, this is the truth. My bias was that I despised the church. In spite of a life-saving conversion, in spite of a wonderful local church where I was discipled and called to ministry, in spite of a wonderful theological and practical education where I was prepared for parish ministry, I hated the local church. The church was at best a necessary evil for me to endure while I went about saving souls for Jesus.

Some of the more cynical might say that my disdain for the church was legitimate. And to some degree the cynics are right. There are so few examples of vital biblical churches in America. I had little to no exposure to a church that functioned with Kingdom purposes and values. Most of my experiences were in churches that often majored in minors and wallowed in minutia.

Some of my more sociologically minded friends might say that my local church dis-ease was a function of my age and demographic crowd. Baby boomers have been called an anti-institution age group, and I am one. My generation is hardwired to be distrustful and skeptical of government, industry, schools, and religious organizations.

A Second Conversion

But something like a second conversion happened for me. Three encounters led me to question my bias. The first encounter happened in 1992 when I was appointed to Christ Church United Methodist, Fort Lauderdale, to serve with Dick Wills. Christ Church was in the embryonic days of her turnaround. God was up to something new in that place, and every once in a while I began to catch a glimpse of a high functioning, biblical church. I could feel a new move of the Spirit that began to confront my deeply ingrained bias against the local church.

Second, I began to hear the stories of congregations that were doing church in a fresh and new way. I first heard of places within my denomination like Christ Church in Memphis, Tennessee, and Frazer in Montgomery, Alabama.

Then my horizons were lifted to places like Willow Creek in Chicago and Saddleback in southern California. Each encounter challenged and confronted my anti-local church bias.

Finally, I began to read the Bible differently. It was as if the Spirit gave me a new set of lenses with which to read. I began to see that I had been guilty of theological shortsightedness. The Bible painted a picture of the local church that is the hope of the world. The biblical picture of the church was of a pure Bride adorned for her Bridegroom, of the Body of Christ functioning symbiotically and effectively for Kingdom ends, of a like-minded people linked together by a common allegiance to Jesus and his Kingdom who worked together for the loving takeover of planet Earth.

God used the church I was serving and other Kingdom-minded local churches and his Word to slowly, yet efficiently, transform my bias. In my heart and mind, the church was no longer a thing of disdain or hate, but rather an instrument of delight and honor. My first conversion was to Jesus and my second one was to his Bride, the church.

Friends, I really love the church! She is no longer a necessary evil for me. Instead, I now am devoted to helping her come alive in all her beauty. I have committed the rest of my life to building a highly vital biblical church that honors God and helps people. If you asked me to name the number one thing I preach and teach on, it's the church. I stay awake at night dreaming of ways to grow a highly vital biblical local church. It's my one driving passion!

And, yet, I am a realist. I understand that leading a church, whether you are clergy or laity, is hard. Some call leadership in a local church difficult and even dangerous work!

Grace at Grace Church

At this writing I am beginning my seventeenth year at Grace Church, a multisite United Methodist church in Southwest Florida. We have four campuses, three worshiping campuses, and a community center. One of the church campuses worships more than 2000, one campus worships 350 and one worships 225. Two of the campuses are "adoption" sites. They were United Methodist churches that, after years of decline, self-determined to become a campus of Grace Church.

The most recent "adoption" campus was the Central United Methodist Church in downtown Fort Myers in a transitioned neighborhood. At the time of adoption, it was an 88-year-old congregation that had had 42 pastors in her history. A group of courageous leaders with a part-time pastor from our staff and a coach from a Christian ministry spent nearly a year building community, discerning their internal and external context, and prayerfully considering their future.

After nine months of regular meetings, this brave group of Central United Methodist Church Christ-followers made a motion at a duly called church conference for the charter of the church to be closed and for them to reopen as a campus of Grace Church. This was a bold move. The day of the vote 40 members showed up at the fellowship hall. The district superintendent handed out the ballots and told them, "There are only two options we can vote on tonight. Either vote to close Central United Methodist Church or vote to be adopted by Grace Church."

I was sitting in the back thinking to myself, "This is a slam dunk! This will be the first unanimous vote in the history of this congregation—40-0! That's what it will be!" The vote was taken, the ballots were collected, and when the district superintendent read them, I was floored. The vote was 23 in favor of the adoption and 17 in favor of closing. I was flabbergasted. I tried to fake a celebrative tone, and then after some pleasantries, I made my way to my car. I sat in the darkness of my Honda, leaned my head on the steering wheel, and wept. I prayed, "God, how do 17 faithful United Methodists vote to close rather than choose a bold, new future?" Although the "adoption plan" had been approved, my heart was broken.

Two years later, I have a better perspective. First, the adoption of Central United Methodist Church, now Grace Church, Fort Myers Central campus, is a miracle to behold. We sent 40 brave missionaries from Grace Church to partner with the two dozen remaining members for a community-focused restart. With our "Grace Church Playbook"[1] in hand, Pastor Arlene Jackson went to be the campus pastor. She is an alcoholic in recovery turned United Methodist Local Pastor and is a courageous firebrand who, along with her amazing team, has been used of God to transform that congregation. From 30 aging white people, in just two years the congregation has become a mixture of more than 200 black, brown, and white people; some are poor and some are rich. In just two years!

Second, time and experience has helped me get my head and heart around the culture of a declining congregation. All three of the church campuses of Grace Church have been turnaround congregations. The Cape Coral campus was in a five-year decline from 575 to 400. The Fort Myers Shores campus had shrunk from 350 to 70 over 15 years, and the Fort Myers Central campus was in a 25-year decline from 350 to 35. Declining congregations have a culture.

Slowly good people just lose their way in a stagnant mixture of typically inward-focused activity until there is little hope of reversal. Over time, all hope is lost, and it just seems better to close than to try again. Now I get it.

Call to Action

In 2010, I was asked to serve on the Call to Action Steering Team. This gathering of United Methodist leaders included bishops, general secretaries, seminary administrators, pastors and lay leaders who love our church. Our assignment was to do the most thorough analysis that has ever been done of a denomination. We would research and study not only the general church, but also more importantly over 32,000 United Methodist congregations in America. We needed professional, objective research experts who could give The United Methodist Church reliable information about what behaviors, or "drivers" as they are called in the research, are present in highly vital United Methodist congregations.

In the Towers Watson research, approximately 15% of the 32,228 churches (4,961 churches) scored high in vitality based on the vitality index. This means that 15% of our churches have figured out some way to remain highly vital in spite of the fact that 85% have not. It means that we cannot lay all the blame for our congregational demise at the feet of the institution of the church.

At Grace Church, I am privileged to work with a lot of addicts who are in different places in their recovery. One of the most frequent addict tricks I see in pre-recovery is "blame transference." I'm talking with Jim, and he's a full-blown alcoholic. He wants to blame his mother, father, siblings, wife, kids, boss, God, and yes, even the pastor for his drinking. It's very sad.

It seems to me that many United Methodist leaders, both clergy and laity, are suffering from "blame transference." They want to blame the bishop, district superintendent, pastor, lay leadership (or lack thereof)

> **In the Towers Watson research, approximately 15% of the 32,228 churches (4,961 churches) scored high in vitality based on the vitality index.[2]**

and yes, even God for their lack of faithfulness and fruitfulness in ministry. "If the bishop would just send me to a good appointmen...." "If the district hadn't planted a church in our city...."

The good news is that at least 4,961 congregations have figured out ways to prevail in spite of our denominational challenges. These congregations are in all settings, (urban, suburban, and rural). They are of all sizes (megachurches, large, medium, small, and even very small). And they are in every part of our American United Methodist connection from Maine to Hawaii and from Florida to Alaska. To me this is hopeful and promising!

Behaviors of Highly Vital Churches

Five behaviors of highly vital congregations will be examined in this book. We will first look at **pastoral leadership** that is growing spiritually and is deeply connected in accountable, Christian community. Second, we will learn about **lay leaders** who are nurtured in their faith, equipped, and released into transformative ministry. Third, we will consider the importance of **worship** that is transcendent, relevant, contextual, and excellent. Fourth, we will look at the importance of building community through **small groups**. Finally, we will consider the essential practice of congregations engaging in local and global **missions and outreach**. The first four behaviors are directly related to findings of the Towers Watson research. The fifth, mission and outreach, was not included in the research as a separate category, because reliable data was not available. That data is currently being gathered by the General Conference on Finance and Administration, and there are already some preliminary results.

I have grounded each congregational behavior in sacred Scripture. Then I root each behavior in the early Methodist movement, a section I call "Turbo-Charging Our Wesleyan Tradition." Finally, in "On the Road to Vitality," I describe what I believe are transferable principles and behaviors that we are constantly working to live out at Grace Church and that I have seen being lived out in other highly vital United Methodist congregations bearing fruit today. Each chapter also includes a story that illustrates an example of a key principle or behavior from another United Methodist church in a different context. And while we all know, and I say throughout the book, that becoming an increasingly vital church takes time, I also know that sometimes it is important to do something immediately. You need to demonstrate (to church members but also to yourself) that something new is happening and you are committed to positive change. So there are suggestions with each chapter for "Quick Victories."

At the end of each chapter, you will find a summary of key learnings from the Towers Watson research. Of course we have more to discover, but it is essential that we take advantage of what we already know can strengthen congregations so that they will become more and more vital.

Craig Robertson, Executive Director of Spiritual Leadership, has been our coach at Grace for the last five years. He has taught us the importance of clarity around principles. When church leaders read a book or attend a conference, they usually learn about the results that a vital congregation is getting. It is natural to think, *Maybe I can get these results if I mimic this church.* Mimicking another church ministry seldom works.

Supporting those results are processes that these vital congregations execute to get their results. Again, it is easy to think that *if I can just replicate the processes in my church, we will get the same result.* Seldom does this happen. But beneath the processes are the principles and behaviors that drive the congregation. For vital United Methodist congregations, these principles are grounded in Scripture, rooted in the early Methodist movement, and then translated into each congregation's unique context with its own challenges and opportunities.

Continuous Improvement

There is one other thing I see vital congregations doing. They slowly get better at what they do. Businessman W. Edwards Deming first introduced "continuous improvement," a business model that transformed Japan's economy and then became a business model around the world. A lifestyle application of this principle is that crash diets don't typically work while slow intentional lifestyle changes do. Cooperating with God's design for proper eating and constant exercise, health can be attained.

The same thing is true in our walk with Jesus. You don't just step over the line of faith, say "yes" to Jesus, and, bang, everything is fixed. The Christian life is a pilgrimage. It's a journey. And that is also true of vital congregations. They welcome feedback. They mine for problems and tirelessly fix them, getting better at the art of ministry, day after day, week after week, month after month, and year after year. After every major initiative at Grace, we gather the team leaders and reflect on how the event went, then we make adjustments that can help us do it better, and finally we list precisely what we are going to do better next time. It's continuous improvement.

Friend, I love the church, and I want to invite you to love the church with me. My prayer is that as you read the pages that follow, you will find your love for the Bride of Christ bringing you to tears and moving you to join Jesus in releasing the Body of Christ into this world of his that so desperately waits to see her beauty!

I.

Spiritual Pastoral Leadership

*So, my child, draw your strength from the grace
that is in Christ Jesus. Take the things you heard me say
in front of many other witnesses and pass them on to faithful
people who are also capable of teaching others.*
2 Timothy 2:1-2

Pastors of highly vital congregations live, lead, coach, and set vision in accountable community.

Throughout biblical history when God wanted to get something done, he would raise up a woman or man who was charged with a God-honoring assignment. . Abram and Sarai obeyed God when they left their people and land to begin a nation whose mission was to bless other nations (Genesis 12). Moses had a rap sheet and was a renegade living on the run. He was tending sheep on the "back forty" when God called him to lead a mass exodus of God's people from the tyranny of Pharaoh's Egypt "to a good and broad land" (Exodus 3:8). The last of Jesse's boys, David, was set aside as the next king of Israel while the first king, Saul, was still sitting on the throne (1 Samuel 16). When God wants something done, God taps someone on the shoulder and says, "I've got a job for you!"

Now these men and women were typically a mixed bag of saints and sinners. They were earthy saints or, as one of my pastor friends, Jamie Stilson says, they were "ugly leaders."[1] Joseph was too immature to handle the dream God had for his life. Ruth could be accused of being co-dependent in her relationship with her mother-in-law, Naomi. Solomon with his 700 wives and 300 concubines would likely have been diagnosed as a sex addict in the 21st century. Timothy wrestled with insecurity as he struggled with claiming his identity as a leader in the early church. God tapped ordinary people to do extraordinary work.

And the job God calls these women and men to do is always a God-sized assignment. It's always a big and daunting job.

"Build an ark!"

"Kill a giant!"

"Have a baby when you're a virgin!"

"Carry a cross!"

"Plant a community of Jesus followers where his name is not known!"

These were no small assignments. When the job gets done, everyone will know that it had to have been God who accomplished it. No human being could ever accomplish the job without huge amounts of divine intervention.

Paul, the great missionary, knew this reality personally. He was a killer of the church who, by the grace of God, turned into a pillar of the church. Paul called himself "the biggest sinner of all" (1 Timothy 1:15). In one of his most important teachings, he describes the kind of people God calls to do his bidding.[2]

> Look at your situation when you were called, brothers and sisters! By ordinary human standards not many were wise, not many were powerful, not many were from the upper class. But God chose what the world considers foolish to shame the wise. God chose what the world considers weak to shame the strong. And God chose what the world considers low-class and low-life—what is considered to be nothing—to reduce what is considered to be something to nothing. So no human being can brag in God's presence. It is because of God that you are in Christ Jesus. He became wisdom from God for us. This means that he made us righteous and holy, and he delivered us. This is consistent with what was written: *"The one who brags should brag in the Lord!"* (1 Corinthians 1:26-31)

Leadership in God's kingdom has always been a daunting task accomplished by less than likely people.

So when the movement of Jesus went viral from Jerusalem to Judea to Samaria and to the ends of the earth (Acts 1:8), God assigned men and women like Paul, Silas, Peter, Barnabas, Philip, and Lydia, with establishing missionary outposts called "churches." Then these apostolic leaders raised up, equipped, and trained "pastors" or "elders" to oversee these fledging communities of faith.

You see this mentoring relationship beautifully illustrated in Paul, the mentor, investing in Timothy, the young pastor in Ephesus.

In the New Testament, pastors had a shepherding role. Peter, the impetuous one (remember he walked on water and cut off a slave's ear) turned radical apostle of Jesus, explained how to be good shepherds.

> Like shepherds, tend the flock of God among you. Watch over it. Don't shepherd because you must, but do it voluntarily for God. Don't shepherd greedily, but do it eagerly. Don't shepherd by ruling over those entrusted to your care, but become examples to the flock. And when the chief shepherd appears, you will receive an unfading crown of glory. (1 Peter 5:2-4)

Peter expected these leaders to lead with great care for the flock, knowing that some day they would stand before the Chief Shepherd. Being a pastor never has been a haphazard vocation. It is holy work to lead and care for the people of God.

That's why pastors then, as now, were charged with a dual task of watching over themselves as well as welcoming being watched over. They are flip sides of the same coin. Pastors had to take responsibility for their own lives as well as invite others to watch over them.

One of my life verses is 1 Timothy 4:16a where Paul writes: "Keep a close watch on yourself and on your teaching" (NLT). I love the way the Common English Bible translates this verse: "Focus on working on your own development." The elder leader, Paul, encouraged the younger pastor, Timothy, to keep an eagle eye over his own life. Paul understood that pastors needed to take responsibility for their own development as followers of Jesus and leaders in the church.

But pastors were not left alone in their assignment of shepherding congregations. Isolation was not an option for first-century pastors. Though the exact polity is hard to trace in the book of Acts and New Testament letters, there was clearly a web of accountable relationships for first-century pastors. They were watched over. Listen to Paul's admonition to Titus about his ministry of teaching: "As for you, promote the kind of living that reflects right teaching" (Titus 2:1, NLT).

Clearly, Paul had relational entree into Titus' life and ministry. This kind of oversight in the early church is woven throughout the book of Acts. Ordinary, earthy women and men were called by an amazing God to lead in a Kingdom assignment. The jobs were always overwhelming. They seldom felt up to it, but this seems to be the way of our remarkable God.

TURBO-CHARGING OUR WESLEYAN TRADITION

I was not born a Methodist. Somehow in the mystery of how God's sovereignty and human free will work, I landed in a United Methodist congregation in the summer of 1978, shortly after graduating from high school. I knew quickly that I was "at home." Pine Castle United Methodist Church was a vibrant, vital congregation with a heart for the lost both locally and globally. They loved the poor and marginalized. Small groups were places of rich community and spiritual growth. Sunday worship included heartfelt, transcendent worship and practical, biblical preaching. I was stretched, challenged, comforted, and healed in that church.

Only years later at Asbury College (now Asbury University) as a Bible major did I begin to learn why my local church behaved the way it did. My pastor and our leaders were thorough followers of Jesus in the Wesleyan tradition. They had figured out ways to contemporize, or as I like to say, "turbocharge," the principles and practices of the early Methodist movement. The movement led by John Wesley in England in the 1700s informed our life together as a congregation.

Thirty-four years after first walking into that United Methodist congregation, I find that the message and the methodology of the early Methodists still meet the deep needs of our world in the 21st century. In fact, the bond is even stronger. Our unique commitment to hold personal piety and social holiness together resonates with the desire that many in our world have to make a real, lasting difference.

At a Jurisdictional Conference of The United Methodist Church, retiring Bishop William Willimon gave the opening sermon, "Come Holy Spirit." Using Acts 1 and the drawing of lots for the replacement of Judas as his text, Bishop Willimon told us that was "the first Jurisdictional Conference." Then he reminded us, as we gathered to elect new Bishops, that The United Methodist Church believes two things to its core. First, Jesus is Lord. And second, preachers need to be watched! That's why they elect overseers. John Wesley believed preachers needed to be watched too.

So it is not surprising that our United Methodist polity includes Episcopal supervision of clergy. This is directly connected to our Wesleyan heritage. We pastors need to be nurtured and shepherded and watched over... with love and grace! Of course, to hold in faithful tension our past and our future has never been easy. Even now, for example, across the United Methodist connection, we are thinking and praying about the nature and length of clergy appointments.

The recent Towers Watson research has confirmed that vital congregations are often associated with longer appointments.[3] But whatever your situation, sisters and brothers in pastoral leadership, I would encourage you to treat every new appointment, especially as senior or lead pastor, *as though you are going to be in that place for a significant period of time.* These are seeds you can plant, in-

---

Setting Goals   Elbert Dulworth, District Superintendent,
                                                               Marquette District

A partnership between lay leadership and the pastor is critical in setting goals, planning and vision.

Significant change can happen when the pastor and lay leadership work together to set goals. I served as interim pastor for two years at a midsize church. The S/PPRC, the district superintendent, and I signed a covenant together that included goals in specific areas of change over our two years together. This painted a picture of how we would move forward together. We had regular updates, and when there was frustration, we could check our decisions against our goals. Were we staying on focus? During the last seven months, we worked especially hard to complete the plan. At the end of our two years, we could look back and celebrate all that we accomplished.

During our time together, when members came to me as pastor with questions or complaints about what we were doing together, we would look at the goals that were set by the leadership of their congregation. There was a clear line of communication to those lay leaders. I reminded them that the pastor's job is to work with the leadership to set clear, specific goals and to lead as the congregation works to achieve them. The ownership of the goals was with the lay leadership not the pastor.

That covenant informed my ministry for coming years. In my next church, we had a longstanding recurring 5-year goal to build a new building. We decided to make that a realistic goal with a time frame. We set a clear purpose for the building itself. We shared how our building would serve the community and how our ministry would change. It became real with an action plan, clear steps, a timeline, and a way to track our progress. In the end, it was *their* project, and I was blessed to share in the celebrations with them.

---

deed must plant, regardless of the circumstances of the eventual harvest.

In my sixteen plus years at Grace Church, I have been asked to move. I've had to wrestle with new ministry opportunities that would give me more prominence and more money. I've stayed because I always sensed that God had more to do at Grace Church, and I wanted to be part of it. I've never regretted staying put!

I am indebted to my friend Jim Harnish, Senior Pastor at Hyde Park United Methodist Church in Tampa, Florida, for his insights[4] about John Wesley's relationship with a Methodist preacher named John Trembath. Reverend Trembath was a gifted pastor who was not being faithful in his disciplines of reading and daily devotions. Over a 17-year period, John Wesley confronted him in several letters, asserting that his preaching was not getting better because he "read so little" and that he could never be a "deep preacher" without meditation and daily prayer. John Wesley's now famous advice is as appropriate and necessary as it was 250 years ago.

> O begin! Fix some part of every day for private exercises. You may acquire the taste which you have not; what is tedious at first will afterwards be pleasant. Whether you like it or no, read and pray daily. It is for your life; there is no other way: else you will be a trifler all your days.... Do justice to your own soul; give it time and means to grow. Do not starve yourself any longer. Take up your cross, and be a Christian altogether. Then will all the children of God rejoice (not grieve) over you.[5]

Wow! Wesley seemed to be on top of his preachers' reading and devotional habits. I find it intriguing that with all John Wesley had to oversee, he spent considerable energy and effort to correct one Methodist preacher. Early Methodists not only believed that preachers needed to be watched but built systems of accountability for it to happen.

One of the hallmarks of the early Methodist movement was this emphasis on mutual accountability. This gave watching over oneself and being watched over "bite and not just bark." Both clergy and laity in the early Methodist movement were passionately committed to being in healthy, holy, and accountable relationships. In the early Methodist system of mutual accountability, questions were asked about the condition of one's spiritual life. The "bands" were the most intimate, same-gender accountability groups of the Methodist movement. These five questions were asked of every member at every meeting:

- What known sins have you committed since our last meeting?
- What temptations have you met with?
- How were you delivered?
- What have you thought, said, or done, of which you doubt whether it be sin or not?
- Have you nothing you desire to keep secret?[6]

This was the "new normal" for the early Methodists. There was nothing abstract or super-spiritual about living into this kind of accountability.

ON THE ROAD TO VITALITY

I believe there are two essential and inseparable commitments that every pastor and every congregation have to say grace over if they are going to be vital: faithfulness and fruitfulness. Here we are talking specifically about pastoral leaders, but the same holds true for lay leaders . Effective church leaders will help each member and prospective member to develop lives that are ever more faithful *and* fruitful.

Faithfulness

If we United Methodists are going to reclaim our dynamism as a movement in the 21st century, we will, as I have said, have to learn to turbo-charge our tradition. According to the Towers Watson research, 85 percent of our U.S. churches are not currently highly vital.[7] In order to help more United Methodist congregations move toward greater vitality, we need clergy who are living richly and deeply in Christian community and who live lives of serious self-awareness and self-discipline.

Eugene Peterson was asked, " As pastor, what is your essential role?" He responded that his task was to show "how the Bible got lived."

> I needed to be a witness to people in my congregation that everything in the Bible is livable and to try to avoid abstractions about big truths, big doctrines. I wanted to know how these ideas got lived in the immediate circumstances of people's lives at work, in the town, and in the family. The role of the pastor is to *embody the gospel. And of course to get it embodied, which you can only do with individuals, not in the abstract.*[8]

John Ortberg's friend told him that his primary job as a pastor is to "experience deep contentment and joy and confidence in your everyday life with God." Ortberg came to realize that "if that's not the main thing—if it's not mostly being rooted in God, then passion actually become a dangerous thing, because then I'll be tempted to try to fake it, to substitute contrived emotion or manipulation for it."[9]

What is the most important lesson I have learned leading one church for sixteen years? **The single most important thing I lead is not my church, but my life!** No one else will lead my life for me. I have to do this myself but within the amazing gift of Christian community. It takes tenacious intentionality to lead your life well.

I was surprised and dismayed to read about a study of 1,050 pastors which revealed that 72 percent of those pastors only read the Bible when they were preparing for sermons and lessons. Just 26 percent of the pastors in the study said that they "regularly had personal devotions and felt that they were adequately fed spiritually."[10] This speaks to the spiritual emptiness of many clergy.

I am susceptible to the same weaknesses and failures as everyone else. So I have built into my life multiple ways to hold myself accountable. I meet every other week with a "coach" via the Internet who keeps me accountable for my life. Craig Robertson, who I mentioned in the Introduction, is an amazing Christ-following businessperson who passionately loves Jesus and the local church. Frankly, Craig wades out into my junk and challenges me to live more passionately for God and faithfully to the mission of Jesus.

I have been part of a covenant group that has met twice a year for more than 20 years and a city pastor's group that has met for more than 16 years. I participate in two men's small groups at Grace Church, as well as a recovery study. My wife Cheryl and I have taken marriage classes, and we have been in therapy to assist us. I tell you these things about my own life in order to emphasize both how important and how challenging it is to liveour lives well, as Christians and as pastors.

Knowing my own need for others to help me live well, I have also built that support into the way we work together as a staff at Grace. We have three church campuses and a holistic ministry center, the Grace Community Center. We have four appointed clergy, two elders, and two local pastors. As the Lead Pastor, I oversee the other three pastors. In order for our relationships to stay healthy and holy, we meet either together or individually for at least eight hours a month. Weekly, I meet with each of them for one hour for what we call "coaching." They bring to our time a completed accountability sheet. It has two main questions with a series of additional probing questions.

Operational Team Accountability Sheet

Name:_____

Date:_____

1. How is it with your soul? Are you abiding in Jesus?

Remain in me, and I will remain in you. A branch can't produce fruit by itself, but must remain in the vine. Likewise, you can't produce fruit unless you remain in me. — John 15:4

1. How is your personal devotional life?
2. How have you denied Jesus this week?
3. How have you glorified Jesus this week?
4. Are you joyful and content?
5. How are your most important relationships?
6. To what can I hold you accountable for your spiritual life?

2. How is it with your ministry? Are you abounding for Jesus?

As a result of all this, my loved brothers and sisters, you must stand firm, unshakable, excelling in the word of the Lord always, because you know that your labor isn't going to be for nothing in the Lord.
— 1 Corinthians 15:58

1. Share a glory sighting.
2. What progress have you made on your work plan?
3. What celebrations and/or challenges do you have with your Operational Team?
    - Staff:
    - Staff:
    - Staff:
4. How is your Guide (Legislative) Team?
    - What have you done to communicate with your Guide Team?
    - What relationship building have you done with anyone on your Guide Team?
5. To what can I hold you accountable for your ministry?

These two key questions get at our walk *with* Jesus (faithfulness) and our work *for* Jesus (fruitfulness). As we have developed trust and love for each other, it does not feel punitive. As a matter of fact, my team would tell you it's life giving. It holds us accountable to our most important commitments.

These spiritual team environments are what keep us going in ministry. In the past five years in my group alone, Pastor Wes's dad died of cancer; Pastor Arlene's sister died on her 43rd birthday; we had to exit one of our pastors in a very difficult situation; and my youngest son, Nathan, has struggled profoundly in entering his young adult years. Ministry is hard. Some would even call it dangerous work. And as leaders, we need to be constantly strengthening our own faith.

I believe this dynamic of leading our lives well and watching over one another was at the heart of the Wesleyan movement that blazed across Great Britain and then jumped to North America, and it can be once more.

Why this strong emphasis on faithfulness? As leaders called to ministry, isn't the need for our own faithfulness obvious? Frankly, it's theological. I have a strong belief in the doctrine of original sin. Left to ourselves, even the most committed and faithful follower of Jesus will drift. At Grace, we like to say that "the drift is always south!" The 18th century hymn writer Robert Robinson said it best in the classic hymn "Come, Thou Fount of Every Blessing":

> O to grace how great a debtor
> daily I'm constrained to be!
> Let thy goodness, like a fetter,
> bind my wandering heart to thee.
> Prone to wander, Lord, I feel it,
> prone to leave the God I love;
> here's my heart, O take and seal it,
> Seal it for thy courts above.[11]

We wander, and we need people who love us and have our best interest at heart to partner with us to be spiritual leaders.

Fruitfulness

As you have seen in the Team Accountability guidelines, faithfulness and fruitfulness are inseparable. While we always begin with intentional focus on our own spiritual lives, that focus always *moves toward and includes fruitfulness.*

I want to share with you some principles that I have learned on our journey toward congregational vitality, a journey that is still very much a work in progress.

I believe that these principles are transferable and can be used in any church that desires the fresh wind of the Spirit to blow through their congregation.

First, **be honest about your current situation**. Just like many human beings, many churches live in denial. Comfortable with the status quo, the church is lulled into believing all is well, when the reality is far from it.

On Tuesday morning of my first week at Grace Church, a bookkeeper who had been hired to balance the checkbook (which had not been balanced in two years!) knocked on my door to share with me that she had finished balancing the church checking account. Becky said, "Jorge, we've got $29.16 in the checking account." I asked her, "What do we owe on the sanctuary?" Becky said, "1.2 million dollars." "How much do the unpaid bills total?" "$20,000." "How much of our apportionments have we paid?" "25 percent." I wanted to call the bishop back and beg for my old appointment.

> *Use your influence to inspire others to get behind needed changes.*

Instead, God gave me the gift of courage. I asked the secretary to call a leadership list with forty names on it and invite them to a meeting with their new pastor. Thirty-eight of them showed up. I shared with them that I believed that God had called me to Grace Church, and that I was excited about our future together. Then I told them the truth, I mean the unedited truth. I told them about the debt, empty checking account, and unpaid bills. The whole "kit and kaboodle."

There was disbelief on many of the faces that night. Some did not know about the debt. So I did what any pastor would do. I passed the plate. I asked leaders to lead. Then I told them about the worship attendance situation. I told them that we had been declining for more than five years and that at this pace we would close the doors and sell the property to the Baptists within ten years. Many were still in shock over the money, and the word about worship attendance was difficult to hear. Yet it was the truth. Like so many congregations, we were in serious decline. It was time for truth telling, not sticking our heads in the sand.

My job that night in September of 1996 was to be lovingly prophetic about our spiritual condition.

The lost were not being reached.
The won were not being discipled.
The poor were not being fed.
The world was not being reached.

And you know what? Nobody got mad. They got sad and then they got serious and then they got busy.

I know being honest about our current reality was a breakthrough point for us. I also think that it is counterintuitive for many pastors. It feels pastoral to "be nice" and offer platitudes about the church, but it doesn't change a thing. Resist it, my friends. Turnaround begins when everyone gets honest and quits playing "let's pretend." Truth telling is one of the gifts that a courageous pastor who wants to lead a congregation toward vitality has to pray for.

Second, **help picture a preferred future**. The self-esteem of our congregation was in the toilet. Yet when I flipped through the pages of the New Testament, I saw a totally different picture of the local church. I saw the local church as "the bride of Christ." I saw the local church as "the hope of the world." I saw the local church as "the body of Christ." I saw a dynamic organism filled with Holy Spirit power, transforming culture, winning the lost, caring for the poor, and reaching the world.

I saw a huge discrepancy between the church I was charged to serve and the church I saw in the pages of Scripture. My job was to help paint a picture of a preferred future. For any organization to get healthy, it has to have a future toward which the entire organization is being pulled. Like a taut rubber band, the preferred future pulls the present reality to it.

Help the congregation see, set, and achieve a biblical vision.

How would I do this? How would I paint a picture of our preferred future? I chose to do it primarily through preaching. I spent the first nine weeks at Grace Church preaching a series I called "The Exciting Church!" The first week, I introduced a biblical picture of the exciting church that was envisioned by the Father, established by the Son, and empowered by the Spirit. Then I asked the congregation to join me in praying, surrendering, and obeying God's will for their lives and Grace Church.

The next eight weeks I spoke on the exciting church where people love, grow, pray, gather, worship, witness, give, and serve. My hope was to re-image the church. My job was to paint a picture of a preferred future that was compelling. I wanted to paint a picture of our future together that was invitational in nature and yet challenging.

The seeds planted over those nine weeks have borne great fruit over the past 16 years. When I came to Grace Church, we had little significant Christian community. I began a men's small group within a few months of arriving. I knew that people would do what I modeled. I continued to speak about the "one anothers" of the Bible and invited our people to "do life together." Today, we have more than 1,000 people in some kind of small group. We have a ways to go, but we are on the right road. The exciting church where people gather has begun to happen at Grace Church.

Teaching our people to do relational evangelism was birthed in those early days. I taught our people the biblical value that lost people matter, that we needed to be the exciting church where people witness. And they began to invite

---

Turnaround   Faith UMC, Fargo, ND

Small Groups are a portal to the congregation connecting with people who might not otherwise engage the church.

In June of 2010 Faith United Methodist Church, Fargo, North Dakota, was 6 months from closing. Seventy percent of attendees were over the age of 70. Today, two years later, only 25 percent of attendees are over 70 with much of the growth in young families with preschoolers. Faith's quick turnaround rested upon the proven principles of strong pastoral leadership by Rev. Kevin Kloster. Kevin cast a vision on his first day that Faith UMC would become the church that people in North Fargo would want to attend. Everything Faith does comes into alignment with that vision. "It's important in churches that are dying to help them see their potential, and then inspire them to want to achieve it and believe they actually can. Pastoral leadership in transitioning congregations must provide vision, motivation, and best practices to bridge the gap between what is and what can be," says Rev. Kloster. At Faith UMC Pastor Kevin accentuated the obvious. "Our doors will close unless we change our focus and ministry toward reaching younger people." With each change came a reason for the change and why it would help Faith UMC become the church in North Fargo people would want to attend. Change usually brings some form of dissent. At Faith UMC key leaders were positioned to listen to the "grumbling" and then rearticulate the sense of urgency in ways people could understand. Faith UMC added a contemporary service to reach younger people; formed an outreach team that, within 4 months, put on an event that brought more than 500 children through their doors; moved out into the community to do acts of kindness for their neighbors; and created an atmosphere of enthusiasm so that people would want to invite others to worship.

---

their unchurched friends. The major evangelistic turnaround came one year after I arrived when we launched our contemporary worship service. That first Sunday in September of 1997, 261 people showed up. It settled in at around 150. Within nine months it was the largest service. On its one-year anniversary, we moved into our sanctuary, and a year later we did the unthinkable. We canceled one of our two traditional services and began a second contemporary service. Since September of 1997 at our Cape Coral campus, we have grown in worship attendance from 500 to more than 1500. And the vast majority are from the ranks of the un-churched, once-churched, or over-churched.

In 2001, our major evangelistic initiative was a recovery ministry. In January 2001, we began Celebrate Recovery, a biblically based, Christ-centered twelve-step recovery service. That service has grown to include a weekly barbecue supper, worship service, small groups, and coffee house. This happens every Friday night. At the same time, we began our immersion baptism services.

Tell your people what God says about them. They are a royal priesthood, a holy nation.

I have baptized more felons, ex-cons, former prostitutes, alcoholics, and drug addicts than you can shake a stick at. This is Kingdom stuff, and it's addictive.

Helping Grace Church catch a vision of who she can be continues to be a major thrust in my preaching. Tell your people what God says about them. They are a royal priesthood, a holy nation. They are the bride of Christ, his hands and feet on this earth. Picture a preferred future and watch the Holy Spirit help them live into their full Kingdom potential.

Third, **practice the genius of the "and" instead of the tyranny of the "or."** In his book *Built to Last,* Jim Collins identifies the differences between A companies and A+ companies. Practicing the genius of the "and" instead of the tyranny of the "or" is one of the principles he discovered in A+ companies. These companies were committed to both customer service and profit making. It was not an either/or proposition.[12]

What does this have to do with moving congregations toward vitality? I often see energized, visionary pastors who land in a new church and hit the ground with both barrels blazing. They want to change the DNA of the church overnight. They go to Frazer Memorial United Methodist Church in Alabama or Saddleback Church in California or Willow Creek Church in Illinois, and they are "good to go." Long-standing committees with entrenched leadership are eliminated, service styles and times are changed, staff is fired and hired, and . . . within a year or two . . . the Senior Pastor is gone too.

What went wrong? Often, it's too much, too soon. It's too many ultimatums. "You change or else . . . ." Instead of raising a new model of ministry while gingerly and patiently dismantling the old model of ministry, this fast-paced, take-no-prisoners approach is used, and in the end, churches are left reeling, pastors are left smarting, and the bishop and the cabinet are left scratching their heads.

Let me illustrate this principle. Like many of us, I inherited several sick ministries. One was a United Methodists Men's group made up of old warhorses. They met on a Saturday once a month for breakfast and a speaker from the community. I went for the first few months, and then began to share with them a new vision for men's ministry. I told them I was going to start a new group for men that would meet once a week at a time when younger men still going to work every day could attend. I did *not* tell the original group that they should or must disband or change their program. Slowly, these guys began to see a new way of doing ministry. The long and the short of it is that this group of men is now a small group that meets alongside a dozen other men's small groups. I minimized the old way while maximizing a new one. Exactly the same thing happened with our United Methodist Women.

I don't want to paint too rosy a picture. Many of my dear friends of the early days at Grace have left the church. In spite of being honest about our present reality and painting a preferred future, in spite of practicing the genius of "and" instead of the tyranny of the "or," many could not handle the change. But for every one who left (most of whom are currently in other United Methodist churches in our area), ten more came. There has been pain. I even caused some of it in my youthful zeal; but for the most part, I think both God and people were honored. Laying down the law doesn't do this very well.

Fourth, **trust your gut**. There is nothing quite like Spirit-led discernment. Dick Wills taught me this. He not only taught it, but also modeled spiritual leadership at Christ Church in Fort Lauderdale. I watched in amazement as he would sense the heart and mind of God in staff decisions, building projects, and new ministry initiatives.

In the fall of 2003, I found myself a bit antsy. The church had grown but was slowing down. We no longer had any seats at our optimum time. Our main campus includes 6.3 acres, and our sanctuary can seat 550-580 people in chairs. At 10:00 a.m. we were worshiping about 525 to 575 every week. You add in about 200 children, and that's all we can handle at one time in the sanctuary, Fellowship Hall, and parking lot. So, I was bit discouraged. Was it time for me to leave?

I met with my district superintendent and shared with her my low-grade dis-ease. I told her I did not want to leave but wondered if I had reached the zenith of my leadership potential. Now you also need to know that I am wired for challenges. They keep me motivated.

As we talked, I threw out the possibility of Grace Church adopting a low-functioning church in a high-growth area. Well, as only the Holy Spirit can arrange things, both my D.S. and our bishop were considering the same possibility. There was a church seventeen miles from us that was struggling. There were about 50-70 people attending weekly. A huge developer in southwest Florida had purchased thousands of acres across the street from it and was beginning to build homes.

We began talking with the church in January of 2004. By February, we came to an agreement on this new initiative. By March, the bishop and the cabinet concurred with my selection of the campus pastor; and by June 15, he was on the property ready to lead the church. We became one church in two locations.

How did it go? In late July of 2004, this little church that had not done VBS in years had fifty children participating in VBS, mostly from the community. In spite of Hurricane Charley's devastation, that fall we began a serious outreach into the community and soon worship attendance had risen to 150-180 up from 50-70. There was the sweet smell of new life at Grace Church, Fort Myers Shores campus!

My mind said this was impossible! My gut said "Go for it!" Listening to the Spirit-led whispers is essential to continuing vitality.

Fifth, **discern your job from the beginning**. I've learned that if you are not clear about this one, other people will tell you what your job is. It will either be a board or a judicatory or the ushers in the parking lot after church.

When I came to Grace Church, I told the Staff-Parish Committee that I had four jobs as the Lead Pastor and that I would try to order my life and ministry after these four priorities.

As I said earlier in this chapter, my first job is to *stay well*. That means staying spiritually well most of all. It means I need time to reflect, read, and rest. I need time for a strong marriage and healthy family. I try to go to the gym regularly and try to stay physically well.

Self-leadership demands rigorous self-awareness. The secret is to not drift into self-absorption. It's not about becoming obsessed with myself, but rather becoming aware enough of myself that I lead out of my God-given strengths with a keen awareness of my hurts, habits, and hang-ups.

My second job is to *preach the best messages I can.* I am still amazed at how many pastors put off working on their messages until late in the week. I have built into my life weekly check points that demand my completion of certain parts of my message by certain times in the week so that our communications staff can get worship folders and Power Points done on time. I have to have my outline to them by Wednesday afternoon. This keeps me accountable to my message preparation pace.

> **Your greatest tool for inspiration: preaching the very best you can every week.**

My third job is to *lead our ministry team.* Our staff has grown from three full-time and five part-time to more than 100 full or part-time employees. Leading this team is not done by accident or haphazardly. It's intentional and planned as well as informal. I have come to believe that the single greatest detriment to our church going to the next level is not about facilities, new staff, or new ministry initiatives, though these are important issues, but rather how I lead. I agree with Dale Galloway that with every 15 percent of congregational growth, a leader has to change how he or she leads. That has been our experience at Grace.[13]

My fourth job is to lead our unpaid servant *leaders.* I spend most of my afternoons meeting with existing and emerging leaders, talking, evaluating, and praying about ministry. As a leader committed to releasing God's dreams in people, I regularly meet with women and men who are trying to figure out what God's next step is for them. My radar is constantly focused on the search for Christ-followers who are ready to step into leadership. We have had a dozen or more people join our paid staff because of this

> **Be a mentor and coach for your lay leaders.**

commitment to nurture leaders and potential leaders. Investing in leaders has paid huge dividends in our church. *(See chapter 2 for more in-depth discussion of working with lay leaders.)*

These four jobs take up about 75 percent of my time. Add administrative duties and pastoral care, and that's my week. Let me say it again. If you don't prayerfully discern your job as pastor, someone else will.

The other thing you must do is **determine what hills you are willing to die on!** As a much younger pastor, I wanted to fight about everything. Growing in this particular understanding may be more a factor of aging and maturing. I'm not sure. I just know that I'm not willing to go to the mat over the color of the carpet or whether the preschoolers use room 5 or 6 at the 10:00 service.

What I am willing to fight for are our vision and values. Letting these slip is paramount to falling asleep at the wheel.

We must keep our compass set on true north. Keeping our temperature red hot for evangelism is worth taking some licks over. Being passionate about excellence or community is worth losing people over. Rick Warren helped me accept the reality that people are going to leave my church. With my staff and lay leaders, I just get to choose the reason why. It's either going to be over the color of the carpet or whether your church will be passionate about reaching lost people.

Choose your battles; play to stay.

I know that at Grace Church I have often given papal edicts that later I had to renege on. I have used word like "never" and "always" that later, with my tail between my legs, I had to repent of publicly. I have pontificated about what we will and won't do in worship, only to find later that flexibility would have been a better approach.

For example, in one of our worship transitions, we did the unthinkable when we moved our 11:15 a.m. traditional worship service to 8:15 a.m. It was necessary as the crowd was down to fewer than 100 adults, while at the 9:45 a.m. contemporary service, there was standing room only. It was time to make the shift.

The morning planned for this transition came. Before what was now the only traditional service at 8:15 a.m., I was making my way through our church foyer when the traditional worship diva of our congregation said to me "Well, are you heading back to put on your robe?" Inside I was fuming. "How dare she tell me to wear my robe! If I want to wear a robe, I will. If I don't, I won't!" It was arrogance on my part. Just then I heard the Holy Spirit clearly. "Jorge, didn't you ask 100 people for whom I died to make the sacrifice of moving from 11:15 a.m. to 8:15 a.m.? Do you think that was what they wanted to do?" I was stunned. I stood there, my eyes filling with tears and then . . . I put on my robe.

I wish I could tell you I was always that attuned to the Spirit's leading. It would be a lie. But I am learning ever so painfully that the smart leader knows what hills are worth dying on and which ones are not. I believe the Spirit will show us if we ask.

Call or email a trusted pastoral colleague *today* and ask if you can have a regular time for prayer and discernment together.

Begin doing an honest assessment of your church.

Research

What We've Learned from Vital Congregations about Pastoral Leadership
Amy Valdez Barker

The Towers Watson Research on Vital Congregations identified the pastor as a key factor in vitality for congregations. One thousand two hundred pastors from highly vital churches across all church sizes across North American were assessed on 14 leadership attributes.[14] Five of those elements affected congregational vitality.

1. Pastors of highly vital congregations focus on developing, coaching, and mentoring to enable laity leadership to improve performance.[15] Seventy percent of the churches with high vitality noted that their pastoral leadership had this focus and is effective. In other words, of the high-vital congregations 23 percent more of their leaders focus on this important element of ministry than leaders of less vital congregations.

2. Pastors of highly vital congregations influence the actions and behaviors of others to accomplish changes in the local church. Seventy-nine percent of the churches categorized as high vitality indicated effective pastors have the ability to influence the actions and behaviors in order to facilitate and inspire change in congregations.

3. Pastors of highly vital congregations propel the local church to set and achieve significant goals through effective leadership. Again, 76 percent of these congregations who rated their pastor effective at setting and achieving goals were highly vital. This attribute is directly connected to the previous two attributes. Pastors must be able to develop, coach, and mentor laity in such a way that builds trust and empowers the community to see a vision and set a plan for the vision that propels the congregation forward toward reaching their goals for this vision.

4. Pastors of highly vital congregations inspire the congregation through their preaching. The research recognizes that both high-vital and low-vital congregations give value to this element. However, 16 percent more of the congregations who rated their pastor as effective in this area were highly vital. In other words, these congregations value inspirational preaching as an indicator of effectiveness for clergy.

5. Pastors of these congregations show a contribution to vitality after three years, and 36 percent of the highly vital churches have pastors who have served more than 10 years.[16]

Of course pastoral leadership includes more than these five attributes;

however, these are factors that were tested and that showed up consistently among highly-vital congregations. There are also a few leadership attributes contributing to vitality that seem to be influenced by region or average worship attendance.

* In the Northeast Jurisdiction, pastors who spend more time on personal devotion and worship have a strong relationship with vitality.[17]

* In the Western Jurisdiction, pastors who lead in the context of their community also have a higher association with vitality.

* In the South Central and South East jurisdictions, the length of tenure of the clergy has a strong relationship with vitality.

* Congregations that have 350+ in average worship attendance have pastors who spend more time on preaching, planning, and leading worship, which seems to have a strong relationship with vitality.

Pastoral Leadership

What is the most important strategic idea I have learned or thought about differently in this section?

_____

_____

What three things will I intentionally work on in the next six months?

1._____

2._____

3._____

Who can partner with me and what will be the time line for first steps on these three ideas?

Partnering with: **By When:**

1._____

2._____

3._____

What is the one thing that I can do today that will create new energy in this part of my ministry?

_____

_____

What from this section gives me hope?

_____

What do I want to share with my team, colleagues or mentors?

_____

_____

2.

Unleashing the Body of Christ

He gave some apostles, some prophets, some evangelists,
and some pastors and teachers. His purpose was
to equip God's people for the work of serving and building
up the body of Christ until we all reach the unity of faith
and knowledge of God's Son. God's goal is for us to become
mature adults—to be fully grown, measured by the standard
of the fullness of Christ.
Ephesians 4:11-13

Highly vital congregations equip and release laity for Kingdom ministry.

One morning I was doing my daily devotions, and I came across these words of Jesus, "I assure you that it is better for you that I go away. If I don't go away, the Companion won't come to you. But if I go, I will send him to you." (John 16:7) It was one of those moments when you think, *I've read the same passage a hundred times before, and I never saw it this way.* Jesus is with his disciples, sharing a final meal together. These words, found in the five chapters in John's biography of Jesus' life, are known as the Upper Room Discourse. John, unlike Matthew, Mark, and Luke, does not tell the story of the last meal Jesus shared with the disciples, but instead focuses on the washing of their feet. He also gives us more rich teachings of our Master in this setting than the other three.

Here's what hit me that morning. If I'm one of the disciples, and I hear Jesus say, "It's better for you that I go away," I'm at least thinking to myself (if not saying to Jesus and the other disciples out loud), "Now wait one minute here, Bucko! We like hanging out with you, Jesus. You keep talking about leaving us, and I for one don't think that's a very good idea."

And I can understand the sentiment. Jesus did some very cool stuff. He healed people of incurable diseases. He had mastery over nature, calming storms with a word and walking on water. Evil spirits obeyed him. Water became wine. A boy's sack lunch fed thousands. And his teaching had the capacity to challenge and even shut up the religious bigots of his day. The idea that Jesus' leaving could be better for the disciples wouldn't have made much sense for me if I had been in the Upper Room that fateful night.

Yet, Jesus said it. So, what gives? Jesus completed his thought by saying that if he left, he would send the Holy Spirit. Throughout John's recounting of Jesus' teaching in the Upper Room, the Holy Spirit is called the "Paraclete," a Greek word that is translated "the one who comes alongside or comes to one's aid." That is why different Bible translations trying to communicate this word use different terms like Companion, Advocate, Comforter, Counselor, and even Friend.

Jesus said if he left, he would send the Holy Spirit to come alongside of the disciples and that this would be a good thing. The longer I pondered this, the more sense Jesus' words made. He was saying that the reason it was a good thing for him to go away was that when he did, the Holy Spirit would reside in them and work through them so that instead of only one person living out the Kingdom, there would be many. What could be better than one Jesus? How about a whole cadre of women and men, young and old, rich and poor, of every tribe, tongue, and nation, filled with God's Spirit and doing God's bidding on earth? Jesus knew what he was talking about, and he was right. Jesus was pitching the idea of the Body of Christ. Jesus could see Pentecost from the Upper Room.

What could be better than one Jesus?

A few decades later, a former religious bigot named Paul (who had become chief cheerleader for the movement of Jesus among the Gentiles) wrote about the church as the Body of Christ. The human body with all its intricate parts was a perfect metaphor to illustrate a diverse, organic movement of Christ-followers who would make the realities of heaven the realities of earth.

> Christ is just like the human body—a body is a unit and has many parts; and all the parts of the body are one body, even though there are many. We were all baptized by one Spirit into one body, whether Jew or Greek, or slave or free, and we all were given one Spirit to drink. Certainly the body isn't one part but many.... You are the body of Christ and parts of each other. (1 Corinthians 12:12-14, 27)

When Jesus told Nicodemus to be "born again," Jesus implied that our relationship with God matures like a human being. My wife Cheryl and I have had the joy of being parents to Daniel and Nathan, as well as grandparents to Mia, Levi, and Seth, and watching them grow through definable stages. Infants become toddlers. Toddlers become little children and so on. Here the unknown writer of Hebrews picks up on stages of faith development.

> Although you should have been teachers by now, you need someone to teach you an introduction to the basics about God's message. You have come to the place where you need milk instead of solid food. Everyone who lives on milk is not used to the word of righteousness, because they are babies. But solid food is for the mature, whose senses are trained by practice to distinguish between good and evil. (Hebrews 5:12-14)

This writer echoes other New Testament letters that challenge the people of God to mature as Christ-followers.

The incubator for spiritual maturity for followers of Jesus is the Body of Christ. Organically, the Body of Christ is designed by God to help foster spiritual growth so that the whole expression of Jesus is declared and demonstrated. Sometimes people will ask me, "Do I need to be active in a church?" They are often surprised by my response. I'll say, "No." Then I pause and say, "But if you want to grow as a Christ-follower, you do!" Local churches are like gyms. You may be able to get in shape at home by yourself, but when you join a gym or exercise with a group of committed friends, you are much more likely to "stay with the program." Local churches are God's instruments to help Christ-followers get in spiritual shape!

TURBO-CHARGING OUR WESLEYAN TRADITION

We have all heard the saying that early Methodists were organized to beat the devil. Long before systems thinking was in vogue, John Wesley and the other leaders of the renewal movement known as Methodism structured the movement around a "flow of discipleship" that mirrored their understanding of grace.

John Wesley was called a "folk theologian" by Dr. Albert Outler, but this did not mean Wesley did not think theology mattered. But it was the living out of theology that mattered most to him. Wesley and the early Methodists focused on reaching the poor and marginalized of 18th-century England. Wesley wanted what Thomas A. Langford has called "practical divinity." So, Wesley's structure was key and flowed from his understanding of how grace works in a human's life. In *The Way to Heaven,* Steve Harper notes that "for each wave of grace, there was a corresponding formative element to connect people to that grace . . . this conscious alignment is one of Wesley's finest legacies to the Christian tradition." [1]

For John Wesley, form followed function. Wesley understood grace in three distinct seasons of a Christ-follower's life. Each season had a unique people, place, and process.

Wesley understood *prevenient* grace as God's wooing grace that draws us into a relationship with God. A dear friend of mine had a grandson who was born very ill and had major surgery at birth, leaving the family unable to hold him until he healed some weeks later. My friend was telling us the miracle of his grandson Paxson's birth, and then the proud Grandpa said, "Paxson is crazy about me. He just doesn't know it yet!" That's prevenient grace. There are billions of people on the planet today who are crazy about God. They just don't know it yet!

Wesley understood grace in three seasons. Each season had a unique people, place, and process.

Because God is at work in every human being, Wesley wanted to create a people, a place, and a process for pre-Christians to gather. The United Society was this place. In 1739, a group of what we would today call "seekers" came to John Wesley, deeply convicted of sin and desiring reconciliation with God. So every week on Thursdays, these "seekers" gathered in the evening, and John Wesley gave advice and prayer. Out of this need, Wesley fashioned the United Societies where "a company of men having the form and seeking the power of godliness, united in order to pray together, to receive the word of exhortation, and to watch over one another in love, that they may help each other to work out their salvation." [2]

The only condition required of those who desire to be a part of these United Societies was "a desire to flee from the wrath to come, and to be saved from their sins."

Justifying grace is saving grace for Wesley. It is the grace of God that puts women and men in a justified or "right" relationship with God. Justifying grace can happen in a moment like it did for Paul on the road to Damascus or it can happen over a season like it did for Cleopas and his companion as they walked with the resurrected Jesus on the road to Emmaus. I often tell our people at Grace Church, "It can be a light-switch moment when in a flash the lights come on, or it can be more like a dimmer switch, an experience that happens slowly. All that matters is that it happens!"

Wesley created the Class Meetings as an environment for women and men to gather and move toward a place of salvation. These class meetings were often led by laypersons who each served as a kind of spiritual guide and shepherd. The class usually included about twelve people, and they met weekly.

Sanctifying grace is the grace of God that moment-by-moment, day-by-day Christ-followers experience as they avail themselves of the "means of grace" and become more and more like Jesus in word, thought, and deed. As Christ-followers learn to cooperate with the Holy Spirit in the gift of Christian community, they can know not only pardon from their sin, but power over their sin.

Wave of Grace	**Wesley**
Prevenient grace	United Societies
Justifying grace	Class meetings
Sanctifying grace	Bands

Bands were Wesley's most formative people, place, and process to help Christ-followers mature in accountable, Christian community. These bands were same-gender gatherings for deeper accountability and discipleship.

It's easy to see that the early Methodists were "methodical" about their spiritual formation. They were systematic, therefore measuring or metrics were a part of their practice. They kept intricate records of attendance at meetings, numbers of new members, and conversions.

ON THE ROAD TO VITALITY

I have heard pastors, consultants, and leaders say, "There's gold in dem' der' pews!" They mean that the people who attend church have financial resources that can be "mined" for Kingdom purposes. And frankly, they are right. There is far too much money in the pockets of Christ-followers (including my own) that is not being harnessed for eternal Kingdom purposes.

But I think there is an even sadder kind of "gold in dem' der pews" that is being left untapped. It's the treasure of laity who sit in church year after year and are never challenged, equipped, and released to do Kingdom work in the church, community, and world. Only heaven knows, how many gifts and graces are left untouched and unused. In far too many churches, laity "sit, soak, and sour."

It was from Wayne Cordiero that I first heard the phrase "dream releaser" to describe pastors, leaders, and churches who unleashed laity to do "the work of serving and building up the body of Christ."(Ephesians 4:12). Pastor Wayne teaches his people that each of them is "a missionary in disguise." Some are missionaries disguised as teachers, and others are missionaries disguised as retired persons, but every one of them is a missionary on mission for Jesus wherever they are.[3]

For a church in the Wesleyan tradition to be a "dream releasing" congregation, it has to, like the early Methodists, organize itself to beat the devil. It has to release God's dreams in people. At Grace Church, we have tried to model this understanding of each "wave of grace" by ordering our ministry around four ministry processes: reach, connect, form, and send.

I spent ten years in Youth Ministry. It was then that I first learned about James Fowler's stages of faith. Fowler's research led him to conclude that many people have definable stages of development on their way to spiritual maturity. In a similar way, Alcoholics Anonymous advocates a twelve-step pattern for sobriety and spiritual growth. Our four defined stages or steps are our best attempt to help people mature from unbelievers to fully devoted disciples of Jesus. You and your congregation will want to create a process that works best in your unique context. My hope is that our pattern at Grace will be of help to you in that work.

Reach Ministries

These are ministries that engage and invite unchurched people in our community to experience the love of Jesus through the Body of Christ. Matthew 22:9 (NIV) is our core text for these kinds of ministries: "Go to the street corners and invite to the banquet anyone you find." Our reach ministries are our best attempts to engage people who are far from God and invite them into the banquet feast that is the Body of Christ.

Who are unchurched people? They are the least, the last, the lost, the poor, the uneducated, the forgotten, the rich, the powerful, the educated, the proud, the discouraged, the hurt, the helpless, the hopeless, and persons without a purpose. They are young, old, and everything in between. Where are "unchurched people"? They are down the hallway, next door, down the block, around the corner, around the world; they are at the local grocery store, in retirement communities, in nursing homes, in schools, in workplaces; they are in the woods or homebound where we can't see them. They are in our community, and they are in your community.

We have discovered four ways to reach people in our community.

❖ *"They come to us"* reach ministries.

For example, at our Grace Community Center we have more than 40 need-meeting ministries like GED, after-school drop-in program for high school students, a community garden, etc. In 2011, these ministries drew more than 26,000 of our Lee County neighbors to the Grace Community Center.

❖ *"We go to them"* reach ministries.

These are reach ministries that seek to build relational bridges with people far from God "off campus." Our S.T.R.E.E.T Ministry takes blankets, health kits, and other items to the homeless camps in our community. We started a weekly worship service at an assisted nursing facility. We participate in community events, such as having a float at the huge Festival of Lights Edison Parade and a tent for our Celebrate Recovery Ministry at the annual county fair. A significant number of people have testified that their first contact with Grace Church was at one of these "we go to them" events.

❖ *"We invite them"* reach ministries.

Here folks experience God's hospitality and welcome through the Body of Christ. These are high invitational events for our people to invite their unchurched friends. Every other year on Maundy Thursday and Good Friday, we host Jerusalem Revisited, a walk-through drama about Jesus' impact on the world. More than 2000 people walk through this event. Annually, we host a Fall Festival that more than 3000 people attend with more than 30 percent of these being unchurched people. We also promote our Christmas/Advent message series and our Lent/Easter services with simple "invite cards" for our people to invite their friends to church.

❖ We engage Grace Church in strategic partnerships.

Our relationships with secular agencies give them exposure to the work we are doing. These include governmental and private agencies for children, counseling, and health.

Reach ministries are all about building relationships and loving people right where they are. You can't engage and invite if you are not willing to love unconditionally and invest in others, by building relationships and providing opportunities to meet individual needs. Ministry is messy, but God turns our efforts into a masterpiece.

Connect Ministries

These are ministries that help people connect to Jesus and the Grace Church family. Acts 2:42, 46-47 is our foundational text for these ministries:

> The believers devoted themselves to the apostles' teaching, to the community, to their shared meals, and to their prayers. . . . Every day, they met together in the temple and ate in their homes. They shared food with gladness and simplicity. They praised God and demonstrated God's goodness to everyone. The Lord added daily to the community those who were being saved.

As we interviewed followers of Jesus in our fellowship, we repeatedly heard how essential relational connections within our church fostered their growth toward and in Christ. This takes huge amounts of intentionality because relationships are complicated and have the potential of becoming really unpleasant.

In my daily devotions, I noticed a pattern in Paul's letters. The thought that unity might be Paul's number one subject matter in his New Testament letters floated through my head. With this new lens, I began to reread Paul's writing, and the argument held. I believe that one of Paul's driving passions was building, protecting, and restoring the unity of the Body of Christ. For example, in Philippians 4:2, Paul singles out two women in the Philippians fellowship who were bickering with one another: "I urge Euodia and I urge Syntyche to come to an agreement in the Lord."

Unity within God's family was that important to Paul. One of the beautiful things about the Bible is that it doesn't pretend the people were perfect. They fought, argued, broke fellowship with one another, and then worked hard at forgiveness, grace, and restoration. The Bible does not candy-coat the hard work of building and maintaining unity. This gives me hope! Recognizing that building unity within our church is a part of our biblical charge, our connect ministries intentionally work toward unity.

We have *four values* that drive these unifying efforts.

❖ *We relentlessly encourage and assist people as they connect with God through a personal relationship with Jesus Christ.* The starting point for unity in the church is shared faith. Men and women who follow the Master together have a common vision for life.

Developing Effective Lay Leaders

Tom Berlin, Senior Pastor,
Floris United Methodist Church, Herndon, Virginia

Changing the organization structure as the congregation grows including shifting of decision making responsibility.

When I began at Floris UMC, we were a worshipping congregation of 300 that over 15 years has grown to 1150. This growth has required an evolution in the ways we plan, make decisions and structure our ministry. The role of strong lay leaders and competent staff have been a major part of this change.

We moved from a few staff and a large Administrative Board to a small Church Council and a larger staff. Many excellent laity who were once attending meetings have been freed to be involved more in direct service. We found that we were more nimble when Council members discerned strategy and vision, staff were entrusted with daily operational leadership, and laity made ministry happen. People are able to be involved in more specialized ministry that fits their gifts and training. Whether focused on our children's home and medical partnership in Sierra Leone, children and youth programs here in Herndon, congregational care, community outreach, or small group leadership, our members are truly the hands and feet of Christ.

Leading and managing change requires establishment of clear roles, authority, accountability and ministry goals. These goals are set in partnership between church staff, Church Council members, and the congregation. We have milestones that we work toward quarterly, annually and over the course of a long-range plan. As a result, we hope to offer Floris members ministry opportunities they find significant and engaging.

The more you trust key lay leadership and church staff to shape and deploy the vision of the church, the more the Lead Pastor has to get out of the way. If a pastor insists on having a hand in everything, his or her need for control will begin to hinder the Holy Spirit. I, for one, am a finite resource, but the body of Christ is far greater than me. Managing these changes over time has raised the level of our conversation, shifted time and energy from the mundane to ministry, and helped to harness great energy for the work of Floris UMC in the community and world.

One of our strategies for connect ministries is inviting people at all thirteen of our weekly worship services to fill out a "Let's Connect" card. These cards are our 21st-century version of the "pew pads" that we used to pass down the rows on Sunday mornings. A "Let's Connect" card gives significantly more opportunities for people to communicate with us their spiritual, emotional, and relational needs. People can declare their desire to make a first-time or renewed commitment to Jesus, inform us of a desire to join a small group, enroll in a short-term class, or join our congregation. Maybe most importantly, our members and guests can share with us prayer requests. These prayer concerns give us portals into people's lives. Weekly, we get a dozen pages or more of vital information that is shared with the appropriate leaders.

Another connect strategy is our prayer ministry at the altar. We intentionally plan worship to give plenty of time for people to be able to respond by walking to the altar rail to pray. The pastor will simply say, "This morning, the altar is open for anyone who would like to come and pray about anything in your life. If you would like someone to pray with you, please lift a hand and someone will do so." Typically, we see dozens of people at every service coming to the altar for prayer. People are led to Christ, anointed with oil for healing prayers, or just comforted in prayer.

Related to this connect strategy are our "Yes Packets." We often invite people to "meet the pastor at the cross" if they want to surrender their life to Jesus. We have a large cross on the right side of the altar where the pastor who taught that morning stands during the altar ministry time. When a person who comes gives him or herself to Christ, the pastor gives them a "Yes Packet." It's a Bible with a DVD on doing daily devotions and other materials to assist the new Christ-follower in growing in Christ. We want to help that person keep saying "Yes" to Jesus!

❖ *We present constant opportunities for people to connect relationally within the Grace Church family.* Our long-term, ongoing home groups are the "bread and butter" of this value. We have also found that sharing food is one of the best environments to help people connect. The Bible is filled with amazing stories of God's activity when people of faith gathered around tables of food. Picnics, camping trips, motorcycle riding, clay pigeon shooting, and karaoke have been strategies that have worked well to create safe places for people to connect with one another.

❖ *We consistently offer opportunities for people to connect with caring ministries to find hope, help, and healing in times of need.* Some of our strategies include healing prayer ministry, Stephen Ministry, Divorce Care, Grief Share, parenting classes, and marriage workshops.

❖ *We passionately provide places for people to connect to and serve within the ministries of Grace Church.* One of our best strategies for this is creating a multitude of "First-Serve" opportunities. Christ-followers want to serve. We often make it really hard in the church. "First-Serve" opportunities are high-grace, low-risk serving adventures. Greeting at an entrance on a Sunday morning or helping get supplies for a children's ministry event can help people "stick their toes in the water" of service. We also created a "Where Do I Fit In?" brochure. This brochure identifies many of our ministries and gives a brief description and contact person in each ministry area.

Form Ministries

These are ministries that help people develop a growing and transforming relationship with Jesus Christ. Isaiah 64:8 is our foundational text for these ministries: "But now, LORD, you are our Father./We are the clay,/and you are our potter./All of us are the work of your hand."

Enlist and engage in towel-bearing service as many followers of Jesus as possible.

The Wesleyan movement had both a heart for reaching lost people and a passion for growing Christ-followers to maturity. Form ministries are our best attempt to help mature Christ-followers for a life of selfless service to God and the world.

Our form ministries also have *four driving values*.

❖ *We relentlessly encourage and assist people to grow in faith and be transformed into the likeness of Christ through personal devotional practices.* Helping Christ-followers discover the discipline of daily Bible engagement is the number-one factor in growing as a Christ-follower. People who connect with God through reading and reflecting on God's Word mature as Christians.

Help lay leaders deepen their faith and become passionate Christ followers.

We call our devotional reading of the Bible program "The University of the Holy Spirit" (UHS). It's in a prominent place on our website (Go to *www.egracechurch.com* and click on Daily Bible Reading.). Seldom does a week go by that it's not mentioned in a message. At least once a year, we devote an entire message to doing daily devotions as well as teaching a one-hour seminar on it.

Another strategy to help our people grow in their faith has been the Walk to Emmaus weekend.[4] In the past sixteen years, we have sponsored more than 650 youth and adults on these transformative weekends. The Walk to Emmaus is a once-in-a-lifetime, 72-hour spiritual experience. Christ-followers come home like John Wesley at Aldersgate, with their hearts strangely warmed. This program has moved them from sitting saints to towel-bearing servants.

❖ *We present constant opportunities for people to be transformed through the Word of God with relevant biblical instruction and experiences.* We offer short-term Bible studies in a mid-week program we call "Transform," Financial Peace University, and Crown Financial studies as well as one-day retreats and workshops.

❖ *We passionately urge the people of Grace Church to form authentic, purposeful, biblical accountability relationships within the church.* "As iron sharpens iron, a friend sharpens a friend" (Proverbs 27:17, NLT). Intentionally helping our people connect in these "sharpening" kinds of relationships is a major focus of our form ministry team.

Some of the intentional and strategic work includes a variety of small groups like home groups, affinity groups, prayer groups, online groups, accountability groups, covenant groups, and Emmaus reunion groups. We also are piloting one-on-one mentoring with experienced spiritual coaches. Throughout the year, we have small-group connection events as well as small-group leader training events.

❖ *We nurture and develop people's passions and gifts to form them into servants and leaders within Grace Church and around the world—all to the glory of God!* Often in the church, we apologize for asking people to serve. "Charlie, if you wouldn't mind and you've got the time, could you ... umm ... might you usher once a quarter?" Our recovery ministry has helped Grace Church unashamedly claim the power of serving. In the rooms of recovery, service is one of her greatest tools. Service gets people "out of themselves." It postures them to model Jesus. As Paul reminded Christ-followers:

> You must have the same attitude that Christ Jesus had.
> Though he was God,
>> he did not think of equality with God
>> as something to cling to.
> Instead, he gave up his divine privileges;
> he took the humble position of a slave. (Philippians 2:5-7a, NLT)

This self-emptying is a challenge and opportunity for every Christ-follower. The wise leader figures out ways for his or her people to practice servant living.

When I first arrived at Grace Church, one of the first people I met was "Rita." Her career was in nursing. Now retired in Southwest Florida, she was a vital member of my new church. I quickly discovered that Rita had two primary gifts and passions. She was an intercessor who loved to pray with and for people, and she had the spiritual gift of healing. God was using Rita as an instrument of spiritual, emotional, and physical healing.

After this discovery, one Sunday early in my ministry, I shared with the church in a sermon about Rita's giftedness. Then I told them, "If you get sick and I come to the hospital, you will say to yourself, 'That was nice. Pastor Jorge came to see me.' But if you get sick and Rita comes to see you, you will get healed. So let me ask you, Grace Church, would you rather feel nice because I came to see you, or would you rather get healed and go home because Rita came to see you?" This is the power of an equipped and a released laity that does Kingdom work!

Several times a years we offer our "Wired" class. This seminar helps people discover their spiritual gifts, their passions, and their personalities and how God has uniquely hardwired each person for service and ministry. My friend Scott was raised in the church. He thought that "ministry" was what the paid professionals did, primarily from the platform. After taking the Wired class, Scott discovered that he had the spiritual gifts of service and helping. His passion to serve by helping single mothers move or hand out bulletins or work in the community garden *were his ministries*. He was serving God! It was a liberating experience for him.

Strong and effective lay leadership builds vital congregations.

I think that one of the main jobs of a pastor is to be on the lookout for potential leaders for ministry. The pulpit sets the culture for this. The wise pastor preaches on texts that challenge Christ-followers to live into the Kingdom potential. He or she also tells stories of women and men within the congregation who are making the move from the comfortable sanctuary seats to places of ministry in the church and community. When this is a normal part of the Sunday morning worship messaging, the Holy Spirit will stir in the hearts of people. They will set appointments to talk with the pastor about next steps into ministry. They will come to the pastor with new ministry initiatives that God has laid on their hearts to begin. The pastor is charged with creating a spiritual environment for the Holy Spirit to work in the lives of his children.

At least once a year at all four campuses, we have a "Ministry Showcase" event where ministry booths from most, if not all, of our ministries are showcased. After a message on serving, Sunday morning attendees are strongly encouraged (some would say guilt-ed!) into perusing the booths and signing up for a ministry or two. The seeds of service are slung broadly on this day.

Another important element for this form ministry value of service is encouraging them and helping them grow as leaders. Annually, Grace Church partners with the Willow Creek Association in hosting the Global Leadership Summit. In addition to "putting on the servants towel" for area churches and ministry, we harness this event for staff and ministry leaders. Every year, our leaders get super-charged for ministry. We also hold annual ministry appreciation events and encourage ministry leaders to do the same for servants working with them.

In the same way that I would not give any of my three grandchildren (all five and under in age) a sharp knife and tell them to run around the house, conscientious church leaders cannot give servants responsibilities for Kingdom work when they are not mature enough for the work. Once I was meeting with a high-capacity leader who had a huge ministry responsibility in our church, and I asked him about his daily devotions. He told me that he read the *Upper Room* daily devotional every morning. I told him that I liked the *Upper Room* a lot, but wondered if ten minutes of a story and a Bible verse was enough for his soul. His ministry output seemed to me to require more spiritual input than he was getting. I suggested to my friend that he had an option. Either he should increase his daily time with God because his ministry assignment demanded it or else resign from his ministry position. He was holding a full cup without a steady hand. Vital congregations figure out ways to help form Christ-like attitudes and behaviors in their people.

> **Vital congregations figure out ways to help form Christ-like attitudes and behaviors in their people.**

We have learned the hard way at Grace Church about not taking spiritual formation seriously and intentionally. Several years ago, we sent two men on a short-term mission team to a remote setting. These men were Christ-followers but had not been vetted or trained appropriately. They wanted to serve in a mission context, and so we sent them. When they got to the mission setting, their lack of spiritual maturity raised its ugly head. These two Christ-followers from our church got in a fistfight. Yes, a fistfight! We now have in our files a letter from this mission organization with a lifetime ban for these two men ever serving in their mission. This was not one of our prouder moments.

A tool we use to help our leaders with this agonizing task of discerning whether or not a person is spiritually mature enough for a ministry context is what we call the "Ministry Maturity Triangle." It's very simple. The higher a person goes up our organization in leadership responsibility, the fewer options they have in terms of their lifestyle. Here's what this tool affirms. It affirms that spiritual maturity matters. Pastors, staff, and key lay leaders need to bear clear witness to a growing, abiding relationship with Jesus Christ. Why? It's because they are at the top of the leadership pyramid. To hand out bulletins, you don't have to be a member or even a follower of Jesus. Now please 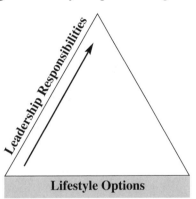 hear me, this is a tool. It's not a stick to hurt people with. We offer lots of grace while at the same time seeking to uphold the importance of having spiritually mature people serving at appropriate levels within our congregation.

Send Ministries

Send ministries release God's people to make the realities of heaven the realities of earth. John 20:21 is our foundational text for these ministries: "Jesus said to them again, 'Peace be with you. As the Father sent me, so I am sending you.'"

Jesus is gathered with his frightened followers after his resurrection. They are still in shock. From alive to dead to alive, Jesus has left his followers a bit bewildered. But here Jesus gets missional! He tells them that in following the resurrected Christ, they are sent ones.

I have often wondered what Jesus' favorite word was. Was it the word *love* because he told us and modeled for us loving God and people? Was it the word *forgive* because clearly Jesus gave forgiveness recklessly to people? In my three-and-a-half decades of walking with Jesus, I am convinced that Jesus' favorite word was *go*. A person's "last words" tell a lot about a person. In all four Gospels as well as the book of Acts, each author is consistent in Jesus' "last words." Look at them with me:

Go and make disciples of all nations. (Matthew 28:19)

Go into the whole world and proclaim the good news to every creature.(Mark 16:15)

...and a change of heart for the forgiveness of sins must be preached in his name to all nations.(Luke 24:47)

As the Father sent me, so I am sending you. (John 20:21)

You will be my witnesses in Jerusalem, in all Judea and Samaria, and to the end of the earth. (Acts 1:8)

Jesus was sending his followers in each of these statements. Going was important to Jesus and to Jesus' followers. The God of the Bible is a missio Dei or missionary God. God "sent" his Son. The Son "sent" the Spirit.

In seeking to be obedient to Jesus' "last words," at Grace Church, we have four send ministry values.

❖ *We prepare and send people into the world globally and locally to proclaim Jesus in word and deed in order to make disciples of Jesus.* At Grace Church, we have created two teams to lead these efforts. We have a Global Send Team that is charged with our international ministry and a Local Send Team that focuses on the ministries in our community.

❖ *We provide opportunities for people to be informed about God's heart for the world.* One of our strategies to fulfill this value is to assign two periods a year to focus on send ministries. In the fall, we have a Send Local Sunday. On this Sunday, we preach on the importance of making a difference for Jesus in our community and enlist our people to give, go, and pray for these community send ministries.

In the winter we have a Send Global Week (Annual Missions Conference). During this week-long emphasis, we bring in many of our global missions partners from Africa, Mexico, India, Nicaragua, Cuba, Costa Rica, and other parts of the globe. These guests visit in our small groups and other gatherings telling their remarkable stories of what God is doing in the world.

❖ *We provide opportunities to instruct people on how to be involved by serving in word and deed and proclaiming Jesus.* Globally, this means we offer Short-Term Mission Team Leader Training as well as Team Training for Short-Term Mission Teams, including teaching on doing daily devotions, fasting, prayer, evangelism, spiritual warfare, raising support, and cross-cultural sensitivity.

Recently, our send ministry leaders recognized the need to train people who serve not just globally but also locally. They are equally important! Our volunteer training includes teaching not only on our vision, values, and strategy but also doing background checks, child protection training, and signing liability waiver releases. We also offer instruction for specific ministries like prayer-team training using Billy Graham's Christian Life and Witness course.

❖ *We provide opportunities to involve people by preparing and sending them to proclaim Jesus in word and deed in order to make disciples.* Our strategy is simple: give, go, and pray. Globally, our people can give, go, and pray for our ten strategic mission partners. Locally, our people can give, go, and pray for our forty-plus ministries at the Grace Community Center.

Connecting the "waves of grace" to our early Wesleyan heritage is also helpful. Our reach ministries create people, places, and processes for prevenient grace to work. Our connect ministries do the same for justifying grace, and our form and send ministries become the environment for sanctifying grace to grow our people.

Wave of Grace	Wesley Group	Grace Church
Prevenient Grace	United Societies	Reach
Converting Grace	Class Meeting	Connect
Sanctifying Grace	Band Meeting	Form and Send

This "reach, connect, form, and send" approach has become part of our Grace Church language. At each campus, posters with a logo from each area is posted with brochures and sign ups. Our worship folders have four sections for ministries to be highlighted. It is our strategy for fulfilling the vision God has given us.

A vital congregation is one that creates incubator-like environments for the Holy Spirit to work God's grace into people.

What "First Serve," (high-grace, low-risk) ministry opportunities can we create to help more lay people engage in ministry?

What will it take for us to start a class on spiritual gifts to help laity discover and be deployed for ministry?

Are our current worship attendance forms telling us all we need to know about members and visitors? Should we design a new form or way of gathering important information?

Research _____

What We've Learned from Highly Vital Congregations about Lay Leadership

Amy Valdez Barker

1. Highly vital congregations have effective lay leadership congregations with effective laity that has a strong impact on vitality.[5] Effective laity demonstrate a vital personal faith, and they rotate leadership. When laity leadership were considered effective, they were 84 percent more likely to be a high vital church, 48 percent more likely to be a high-attendance church (in comparison to membership) and 54 percent more likely to be a high-growth church.[6]

2. In highly vital congregations, effective laity demonstrate a vital personal faith. Sixty-one percent of highly effective lay leadership demonstrate a vital personal faith through regular disciplines of prayer and Bible Study, regular attendance of weekly worship, proportional giving, participation in mission opportunities, and sharing their faith personally.[7] This "effectiveness of laity" coincides with our Wesleyan understanding of the means of grace. It is directly linked to our theological understanding of works of piety and works of mercy that more deeply connect us with our Creator.

3. In highly vital congregations, effective laity rotate leadership. Seventy-seven percent of highly effective laity in leadership share their opportunities to serve with others. This too is not new to the Methodist way of being.

4. A critical mass of effective laity impacts vitality. Fifty-three percent of the congregations that rated favorable on lay leadership effectiveness had more than 50 percent of their worship attendees who have served as leaders in the past five years.[8] This is directly linked to the previous factors affecting vitality. Congregations that equip, empower, and invite laity to deepen their personal relationship with Christ have laity who are willing to serve and share those opportunities with others. Effective lay leadership impacts vitality in congregations both quantitatively and qualitatively.

Keep in mind it is the collection of these elements that affect vitality. Aiming toward having all of these factors will affect vitality in congregations and increase effectiveness.

Lay Leadership

What is the most important strategic idea I have learned or thought about differently in this section?

_____

_____

What three things will I intentionally work on in the next six months?

1._____

2._____

3._____

Who can partner with me and what will be the time line for first steps on these three ideas?

Partnering with: **By When:**

1._____

2._____

3._____

What is the one thing that I can do today that will create new energy in this part of my ministry?

_____

_____

What from this section gives me hope?

_____

What do I want to share with my team, colleagues or mentors?

_____

_____

3.

A People Made for Worship

*So let's continually offer up a sacrifice of praise through
him, which is the fruit from our lips that confess his name.*
Hebrews 13:15

**Highly vital
congregations
have worship that
is transcendent,
relevant, contex-
tual, and excellent.**

A t its core, worship is about the wonder of worshiping the Creator of the Universe before
whom we stand in reverence and declare, "O My
God!" This is not the casual OMG, which has
become part of the language of texting.

David was Israel's reluctant second king. Born
the last of Jesse's sons, David was more comfortable
with sheep and songwriting than with his role as king and leader. After a tragic
series of events with the first king of Israel, Saul, David ascended the throne.
Jerusalem was then made the capital of the nation of Israel. David's first task
was to get the Ark of the Covenant to Jerusalem. As you know, the Ark represented the presence of God to Israel. As the men of Israel wheeled a cart car-
rying the Ark into Jerusalem, the scripture shows us David's exuberant,
worshiping heart.

> David and all the house of Israel were dancing before the LORD with all
> their might, with songs and lyres and harps and tambourines and castanets
> and cymbals. (2 Samuel 6:5, NRSV)

What a picture! David, in the words of Charles Wesley, is "lost in wonder,
love, and praise." Worship for David was not haphazard or reluctant . It was an
experience of his total being.

I have found that there are four ways to help the people in our churches be worshipers who themselves get "lost in wonder, love, and praise." It's interesting to note that in Hebrew "worship" and "work" come from the same root words. Worship is work, but it is a certain kind of work.

First, worship is physical work. Both Old and New Testaments show people worshiping with their entire beings. For example, 2 Samuel 6:14 tells us that "David , dressed in a linen priestly vest, danced with all his strength before the Lord." David worshiped with all his might! Worship involves the body. The Bible does not paint a picture of worship in which the spiritual is somehow separated from the physical. The Bible teaches an integrated approach to worship wherein the spiritual and the physical work in harmony with one another.

Raising our hands, clapping, kneeling, standing, and lying on our face are physical reflections of a spiritual expression to our God. Often when I lift my hands to God in worship, I am telling God I need him. Sometimes, I am trying to express my surrender to him.

I remember a few decades back going to a Billy Joel concert in Miami. It was amazing. The last song he sang was his famous ballad, "Piano Man," in which he sang, "We're all in the mood for a melody, and you've got us feeling all right!" Like the 15,000 people in the arena, I was caught up in the moment. My hands were raised, and my voice was raised. I was swaying back and forth, and then the thought hit me. This is what God wants our worship of him to be like. Worship should engage our bodies.

Does that mean every highly vital congregation needs to worship exactly as we do at Grace? Of course not. But I do believe that worship should involve the whole person. I think it is essential that people engage and respond, not just observe in worship. What might worshiping with your entire being look like in your church?

Second, worship is emotional work. Emotionless worship is an oxymoron. They are two words that don't go together. Look at David and the people in 2 Samuel 6:15, "So David and all the people of Israel brought up the Ark of the Lord with shouts of joy and the blowing of rams' horns" (NLT). Shouts of joy!

God invites us to worship him in stillness too.

Our faith is a faith that is expressed through the full range of human emotions. God made us to experience and express joy and sorrow, mountaintops and valleys. In Psalm 131:2 (TM), Eugene Peterson paints a picture of quieter emotions beautifully. "I've kept my feet on the ground. I've cultivated a quiet heart. Like a baby content in its mother's arms."

Sometimes our worship is climbing up into the arms of a loving God and resting. God invites us to worship him in stillness too. Worship engages the full gamut of our emotions.

Third, worship is financial work. "They brought the Ark of the LORD and set it in its place inside the special tent that David had prepared for it. And David sacrificed burnt offerings and peace offerings to the LORD (2 Samuel 6:17, NLT).

The Ark is placed in a tent and then animal and grain sacrifices are made. What this means is that the people took from their agricultural earnings and gave them to God as an expression of worship. Again, to be true to the entire Bible, you cannot separate the spiritual and the material. Worship is holistic.

Several months ago I was in a worship service where the worship leader was remarkable. He knew how to help engage people in moving from being spectators to participants. As we were singing some old hymns of the church in a new way, I lifted my left hand in adoration to God while I kept my right hand in my pocket. I noticed that my right hand was gripping my wallet. Then I heard a whisper from the Holy Spirit. "Jorge, tell my precious people at Grace Church that I love how they worship me. They love me. They praise me. But many are also holding onto their money." I wept, as I knew God was not speaking just to my congregation but to me as well. More than I care to admit, greed infects my heart and life. Worship also means engaging and responding with the financial resources that God has placed in our hands.

Finally, worship is sacrificial work. "When he had finished his sacrifices, David blessed the people in the name of the LORD of Heaven's Armies. Then he gave to every Israelite man and woman in the crowd a loaf of bread, a cake of dates, and a cake of raisins" (2 Samuel 6:18-19, NLT).

Worship, for David, had moved from the physical to the emotional to the financial, and now to his ministry. What did David do? He blessed people with food. He saw the needs of the people, and he responded. For worship to go full circle, it means seeing people in need and responding. The real test of whether or not you have been with God has nothing to do with what happens in this place of worship. The real test is what happens when you get home. It's how you treat your spouse, roommate, children, neighbor, or friends. It has to do with your treatment of the poor and the needy. This is where the rubber meets the road for you and me.

Biblical worship is holistic. Years ago, I heard a story about an educated and sophisticated college student who went to the backwoods of the country to visit his elderly grandmother. On Sunday morning, she woke the young man up and said, "So, we're going to church." Church was not a part of this man's regular life and experience; but out of reverence for his grandmother, he dressed and joined her in worship. The little country church was Pentecostal in nature with lots of loud singing, foot stomping, hand clapping, and shouts of "Hallelujah" and "Praise the Lord." The young man had never experienced anything like this up close and personal.

On their way home, he asked his grandmother, "What was all that jumping and shouting about back at church, Grandma?" To which the wise grandmother responded, "Sweetie, it's doesn't matter how loud they shout or high they jump. What matters is what happens when their feet hit the floor." Grandma was right! Genuine worship is what happens when we move from the seats to the streets.

Each Sunday, let's ask ourselves, "How has this worship experience changed the hearts, minds, and *behavior* of the participants?"

TURBO-CHARGING OUR WESLEYAN TRADITION

We are in the stream of the Jesus movement that traces its roots back to John and Charles Wesley. Methodists were once known as "shouting Methodists," or as I like to say, "We Methodists were Pentecostal before Pentecostal was cool!"

Music in Worship
Look at how John Wesley instructed the first Methodists to sing[1]:

> Sing lustily and with good courage. Beware of singing as if you were half dead, or half asleep; but lift up your voice with strength. Be no more afraid of your voice now, nor more ashamed of its being heard, than when you sung the songs of Satan.

> Sing modestly. Do not bawl, so as to be heard above or distinct from the rest of the congregation, that you may not destroy the harmony; but strive to unite your voices together, so as to make one clear melodious sound.

> Above all sing spiritually. Have an eye to God in every word you sing. Aim at pleasing him more than yourself, or any other creature. In order to do this attend strictly to the sense of what you sing, and see that your heart is not carried away with the sound, but offered to God continually; so shall your singing be such as the Lord will approve here, and reward you when he cometh in the clouds of heaven.[1]

Ours is a heritage of worship that is heartfelt, joyful, and focused on God! The early Methodists took seriously the "continual sacrifice of praise to God" (Hebrews 13:15, NLT).

Yet, we have to remember that the early Methodists were an evangelical movement within the established Anglican Church. Methodists were and are "mutts" when it comes to theology and practice in worship. There was a commitment to both an evangelical and catholic spirit. Wesley was vigilant in his commitment to the Anglican Church. The "movement" dynamic of the early Methodists makes finding a truly Methodist worship form difficult. I believe this can be a strength in our highly diverse world. Our worship "stretch" is from the dusty holiness camp meetings to the high Anglican cathedral. We are at home with Pentecostal and Taizé worship.

Charles Wesley put the theology and practice of the early Methodists to music. In the hymn "Love Divine, All Loves Excelling," Charles describes the Methodist commitment to holiness of heart and life:

> *Finish, then, thy new creation;*
> *pure and spotless let us be.*
> *Let us see thy great salvation*
> *perfectly restored in thee;*
> *changed from glory into glory,*
> *till in heaven we take our place,*
> *till we cast our crowns before thee,*
> *lost in wonder, love, and praise.*[2]

In "A Charge to Keep I Have"[3] Charles reminds Methodists that they are a people who have joined Jesus in his mission on the earth:

> *To serve the present age,*
> *my calling to fulfill;*
> *O may it all my powers engage*
> *to do my Master's will!*

The music of early Methodists confirmed their calling and served as their marching orders to be a movement of personal and social holiness.

Preaching

John Wesley believed profoundly in the power of preaching as well. Nurtured in the parsonage of an Anglican priest, preaching was properly done in church sanctuary or chapel. But after his heart-warming experience at Aldersgate, in a desire to reach the poor, the marginalized, and the addicted, he turned to field preaching. About his "conversion" to field preaching, he said, "Field preaching was therefore a sudden expedient, a thing submitted to rather than chosen."

> At four in the afternoon, I submitted to be more vile, and proclaimed in the highways the glad tidings of salvation, speaking from a little eminence in a ground adjoining to the city, to about three thousand people. . . . What marvel the devil does not love field preaching! Neither do I: I love a commodious room, a soft cushion, a handsome pulpit. But where is my zeal, if I do not trample all these underfoot in order to save one more soul?[4]

Wesley could not and would not allow the trappings of a comfortable and safe chapel to keep him from fulfilling a greater mission. These are our roots as followers of Jesus in the Wesleyan tradition. When we allow the trappings of "proper" worship (whatever that means) to hinder the Gospel, we step outside our rich, radical heritage.

It is difficult to remain vigilant over years in ministry, to continue to examine our own motives, our rationalizations. I struggle against it, but I am human and therefore "prone to wander." Are you? When that happens, let us confess and begin again.

ON THE ROAD TO VITALITY

Soren Kierkegaard was a great theologian who was born in Copenhagen in the early nineteenth century. He wrote on many subjects related to the Christian life, but nothing in my estimation was more profound than his thoughts on worship. As if he were living in the 21st century, Kierkegaard was critical of worship that focused on performance. To him, worship was not about what happened on the worship platform alone.

He spoke of worship as drama. His analysis was that worship in his day had deteriorated to be a production in which the pastor and other worship leaders had become actors who were directed by God, and the congregation were the passive observers. Kierkegaard suggested that the proper understanding of the worship drama was to see the pastors and other worship leaders as directors of the drama, with the audience as the actors and God alone as the audience.

The Christian band Big Daddy Weave has a song entitled "Audience of One." It seems to me that for worship to be for an "Audience of One," it has to be transcendent, relevant, contextual, and excellent.

Transcendent Worship

Here's what life and the Bible have taught me. God is working in the world trying to draw all people into a relationship with him. The creation itself bears

---

Considering the Context of Worship
Jacob Armstrong, Provident UMC, Mt. Juliet, TN

Worship style isn't always what you envision but has to be what connects with the community. Jacob describes what he imagined worship would be like in an edgy new church plant.

When I was appointed to pastor a new church start, I began to dream of what "my" new church would look like. By the time I hit the ground as pastor of a church with no name, no building, and no people, I had a clear vision of what worship would look like: what we should do and how we should do it. In a few short weeks, though, I realized my vision (though great, I am sure!) did not exactly fit the mission field. As a 27-year-old, I may have desired one type of music, but the community around me would connect more with another kind. The type of clothing that I might have hoped would be "cool" to wear in worship would only be comfortable for a small segment of the people that God had sent me to serve.

This led us into a season of listening to our community. We needed to hear from them. Intentionally listening to our community meant careful observation and open conversation that allowed us to hear the felt needs of the community (which would later inform our topical preaching series) and to understand the culture of our neighborhoods (which would help us know how to choose relevant language, music, and dress for worship). The message of hope in Jesus would be the same, but our community taught us what language to speak so they could understand it. This did not mean an abandonment of what we often think of us as traditional. In fact, we found in our context that the ancient forms of religion would speak strongly to those who feel disconnected from God in our community.

I learned that no matter how compelling the vision may be, it must connect with the people whom God has sent you, or it is a vision that will not live. New churches and old churches alike must desire God's vision instead of our own, and I believe God's vision will always lead us to reach the people in the neighborhoods around us.

the fingerprint of God. Trees, rivers, rocks, and animals all witness to God. But it goes even further. In the heart of every human being is what N.T. Wright calls an "echo of a voice"[5] that something is amiss in the world and in our lives. Augustine said that "our hearts are restless until they rest in Thee" and Pascal called it "the God-shaped vacuum." It's the deep inner angst that was placed in the human heart by God, the hunger to connect with God.

When a person, regardless of his or her spiritual condition, walks into a church, God has already been at work in that person's heart. In our Wesleyan tradition, we call this "prevenient grace." What happens in the next hour to hour-and-a-half in the sacred space we often call the sanctuary will either facilitate the wooing work of God or hinder it. Pastors and other worship leaders are charged with the sacred task of creating a transcendent environment for the Spirit of God to work. At Grace Church, I often tell our worship leaders that we set the table and God serves the meal. The kind of meal we get depends on the kind of table we set. Is it going to be a picnic or a banquet? Will it be finger food or a five-course meal?

The wise pastor and worship team carefully craft weekly worship environments. For more than a decade, we have had a Creative Team made up of pastors, staff, and laity who meet to plan what we call worship "enhancements." These enhancements include dramas, testimonies, props, videos, graphics, and power-songs (songs at the end of sermons). Our goal is to enhance or boost the worship space and experience without robbing the service of its focus on the Triune God.

Several times a year, we have what we call "enhanced Communion services." On these Sundays, we try to slow down our Communion service. I think that the Lord's Supper is often "tacked on" to the end of the message and is rushed. One of my most favorite enhanced Communion services was when we gave everyone a piece of broken tile as they entered the sanctuary. We asked them to hold it in their hand as I gave a message on brokenness. The central point of the message was that through the brokenness of Jesus on the cross, our brokenness is healed. We had stationed four crosses around the Sanctuary and after the message, we invited our people to lay their brokenness before the cross and then receive the Communion elements. It was an exchange of sorts—their brokenness for the healing of their lives through the brokenness of Jesus. The sense of awe and wonder in the sanctuary was palpable. People knelt at the altar after receiving the elements and wept as the Spirit of God swept across their lives.

Several months later at another enhanced Communion experience, after I gave a brief Communion message, I unveiled a 3-by-5 foot picture of hands forming a piece of pottery made from the broken pieces that had been laid at the cross months before during Communion. An artist in our congregation painstakingly made this piece of art as an offering to God and gift to our congregation. I told our people, "God takes our brokenness and makes something beautiful out of it." Once again, the presence of God was "strong in the house."

End your worship service with some "percolating time" for meditation, prayer, an invitation to kneel at the prayer rail with a pastor or lay leader, whatever might work in your church.

Think about some ways in which you might enhance your Communion services. Can you shoot an onsite Communion meditation from a local bakery or a food pantry to connect with the rich meaning of the Lord's Supper? Or hand out 3-by-5 cards and ask each person to write some words of confession, which they will drop in a basket as they come forward to receive Communion.

Another way we try to help people connect with God is to plan our worship so that there are 10 minutes at the end of the service for what we call "percolating time." This allows for prayerful response by the congregation. In our context, we open the altar for people to come and kneel in prayer. If they want someone to pray with them, they can lift a hand, and a trained prayer partner will pray with them.

Sometimes, the teacher will simply lead the congregation in a prayer exercise. If the message is on surrender, an invitation to stand, close your eyes, and raise your hands while repeating a prayer might be given. Soft keyboards play behind the teacher's voice to help foster a mood of intimacy with God and one another.

As I said in chapter 2 (see p.52), we have added a very intentional evangelism call at the end of our worship experiences. Worshipers are invited to come forward and meet a pastor at a large cross and surrender their lives to Jesus.

Some people come to worship at our churches with a deep awareness of their need to connect with God. Some people come to worship at our churches without this awareness, but with a very real need to make this union. Our sacred assignment is to create the environment for transcendent worship experiences.

Is the worship experience in your church transcendent? I encourage you to experiment. It doesn't have to be a huge change, but try something different. Include key lay leaders in your plans and then ask them to help you assess the results.

Relevant Worship

Relevance is a moving target in our contemporary culture. Because of the Internet and social media, the speed of information transfer is down to the millisecond. But when I talk about relevance in worship, I do not mean relevant information, but rather relevant knowledge. Our world has lots of information. From Google to Wikipedia, we can find tidbits and facts about just about anything we can imagine. But what the human heart needs is knowledge, and I believe the best knowledge is found in the pages of sacred Scripture.

That is why teaching from the Bible is essential to a vital congregation. Pre-Christian, new Christians, and seasoned Christians hunger for clear teaching that addresses the issues of their lives. Vital congregations figure out ways to communicate the Bible for life transformation.

When we added our third campus, I wondered about the wisdom of having three pastors each working on a message for his or her individual campus. I formed a Teaching Team made up of the Campus Pastors and other leaders in our church with the spiritual gift of teaching, plus a few of our Worship Pastors. Because I have the spiritual gift of teaching as well as more preaching experience (but not because I'm the Lead Pastor), I lead the Teaching Team.

Put time into well-planned, topical worship series. If you don't have a planning team, work together with pastors from nearby congregations.

Twice a year, we have a Teaching Team retreat to plan our message series for a six-month period. In October, we plan for the following January to June, and in April, we meet to plan for July to December. This is an all-day planning session. Before this day, for several weeks in a row during Sunday worship, we ask our people to give us topics that they would like us to preach on. The list is fodder for this planning day.

At this biannual retreat, I share with the team what I call our "Stuff to Consider" list.

1. Is this a Reach, Connect, Form, or Send series?
2. Rotating pastoral and prophetic series
3. Rotating thematic and expository series
4. "Will You Grow?" (stewardship) emphasis in fall
5. Liturgical calendar (reinventing and turbo-charging it)
6. Growth through big days
7. Enhanced Communion Experiences
8. "Cushion" weekends for campus specific messages

We also review key thoughts I have selected from Adam Hamilton's book *Unleashing the Word*.

These two tools along with the topical list of what our congregation gave us help set the stage for a full day of creative and innovative planning. After six hours of filling up page after page of flip charts, we settle on the five to six series of messages.

Our weekly sermon preparation schedule begins each Tuesday when the whole teaching (preaching) team meets for two hours to draft an outline for that week's sermon. On Wednesday morning, I lock myself away in my office and write from 8:00 a.m. until noon. I can usually write a 6-to-7 page manuscript in that time. I forward the manuscript to each of the Campus Pastors who then revise the manuscript so that it reflects their "voices." They in turn send their final manuscripts back to the other three teachers by noon on Saturday. What this means is that each of us has four manuscripts (remember we have four campuses), and we can each "cherry pick" good stuff for our own sermon!

> **Many of you are leading a church with a much smaller staff. But some things are the same. Planning several months ahead is essential. Don't let yourself become a victim of daily crises.**

It is in just the last four years that we have moved to this team method, and we find that it helps everyone at many levels. First is an economy of work. If each Campus Pastor had to write his or her own sermon from scratch, we have calculated it would be a total of about fifty total hours of work time. Using our method, our total investment of time is about twenty hours. This frees thirty hours a week at each campus for other leadership and pastoral duties.

Second, we have found that this method helps everyone get better at the fine art of preaching. Several of our Sunday morning teachers are staff and laity who have limited experience but have given evidence of the spiritual gift of teaching. The synergy in our Teaching Team helps all of us grow in our capacities.

Third, this method of team teaching has helped us create a "bench" for potential future Campus Pastors or staff members. Our Tuesday Teaching Team serves as a kind of "farm league" for us to develop and release teachers within our congregation.

Many of you are leading a church with a much smaller staff. But some things are the same. Planning several months ahead is *essential*. Don't let yourself become a victim of daily crises. (Are you the *only* person visiting hospitals and nursing homes? Invite a lay person to join you and then go in your place some of the time.) What can you do to give yourself more planning time? Schedule lay leaders to preach? Invite a retired pastor to preach? Talk with your D.S. about the challenge. Schedule a time to meet with other pastors in your district, either online, by conference call, or in person. While each sermon and sermon series will be tailored to the specific context of your congregation, there is a great deal that can be shared and developed together.

Let me also say something about vulnerability and preaching. There was a day in American Christianity when pastors lived their lives cocooned from the congregations and communities they served. It was often called the "glass bubble." Culturally, it seemed appropriate. In an age of blatant voyeurism, appropriate vulnerability on the part of a communicator is essential. Churched and unchurched Americans will not value preaching that is staid and distant.

I think the imperative word is "appropriate." People regardless of their spiritual status connect with a communicator with whom they can identify. At Grace Church, I have found that the bandwidth for heart-to-heart connection from pastor to people is very wide. Struggles in marriage, addictions, and financial hardships are all fair game in our congregation. The stodginess of the cleric goes away when he or she can admit to his or her own journey. A good litmus test for whether a personal story is appropriate is to ask the simple question, "Am I telling this story for the glory of God or some other reason?"

Let me say one final word about relevance in worship. Ours is an educated clergy force. Seminary has equipped pastors to think deeply about many of the ills that infect our church and culture. I have noticed that clergy armed with a seminary diploma sometimes have an "ax to grind" about some cultural issue or personal agenda that leaves a congregation reeling. Preaching prophetically is important. Challenging bigotry and indifference is a role of a preacher, but I do believe that we have to earn this right in a congregation.

In the last several years, my heart has been awakened to the need for Christians to address systemic evil in their community through biblical justice. Our leaders began meeting with a newly forming interfaith group to organize our congregations for the work of justice. To introduce this new accent to our ministry, the Teaching Team planned a five-week series we entitled "And Justice for All?" During this series, we would preach for five weeks from the book of Exodus using the backdrop of Egypt's cruelty as a model for doing biblical justice. I knew that members and guests might confuse this ministry with some political agenda. But it was a calculated risk. A few did get mad and even left our church, but we sensed the leading of the Spirit in this initiative. Here's my point. We did not preach this series and launch this ministry in year one.

Contextual Worship

Part of my assignment in communicating the Bible is to carefully investigate the historical and cultural context of the verses I am studying. Careful interpretation and application of the Bible flows from thorough investigation of the biblical context.

When it comes to worship, particularly in the North American mainline church, we often do not follow this pattern of careful contextualizing. Much of our music, liturgy, and preaching fit the post-World War ll age but frankly miss the mark of the post-modern culture of the 21st century.

Grace United Methodist Church was planted in 1978 in what were then the far northlands of Cape Coral. The average age in Cape Coral was 68. The definitive history book on Cape Coral is entitled *Lies That Came True*. It tells the story of two brothers who bought 100 square miles of mostly marsh land, developed the property modeling it after the canal properties of Fort Lauderdale, , and sold off lots primarily to Midwesterners who would travel south down I-75 to southwest Florida. Cape Coral was a "Mecca" for young retirees.

By the time I arrived as a first-time lead pastor in 1996, just eighteen years later, the average age in Cape Coral had dropped to 38! Young families discovered you could buy a 4-bedroom, 3-bathroom home on a canal with a pool for $125,000, and they were coming by the car load.

Grace Church in 1996 looked like the church that had been planted in 1978. We were primarily a young retiree church. At 36, with elementary and middle-school-aged sons, my family was a part of a smaller population in our congregation. The worship wars were in full swing in mainline Christian denominations in 1996. Horror stories were emerging about the blood baths that were occurring as Baptists, United Methodists, and Lutherans were bringing drums and video screens into sanctuaries. I wanted to avoid this.

To have a "future with hope," we had to offer worship services that spoke the "heart language" of a younger generation.

Years before, I had heard Bill Easum say that to avoid the worship wars, you needed to appeal to grandparents and their love for their grandkids. That the children of seniors in our church left church when they went off to college and got married saddened many aging parents. But seniors not seeing their grandchildren in church was destroying them. As a grandparent today, I understand this sentiment. Easum encouraged us to appeal to grandparents' love for their grandkids. And that's what I did at Grace Church.

I knew that for Grace Church to have a "future with hope," we had to offer worship services that spoke the "heart language" of a younger generation. This meant contemporary worship. I went to one of the patriarchs of our church who had children and grandchildren in our church. I asked him, "Will you pay for and pray for ministry that you don't understand or like if it will get your grand-kids to come to church?" He said, "You bet!"

That man became one of the chief advocates for the transitions in worship that would take place over the next four years. The first year, we didn't make any major worship changes except that we tried to make our 8:30 and 11:00 a.m. traditional worship better. Hymns that people knew were sung. The choir sang music that was meaningful. The hunger for God was palpable in that first year. I was raised in a tradition that "opens the altar" for prayer after the message. Every Sunday, people would slip out of their seat and kneel for a time of prayer. This alone changed the worship culture.

Within a few weeks of arriving, the staff and I decided that starting a 9:45 a.m. contemporary worship service would help us join Jesus in his mission in our community. In our worship folder we printed "9:45 Contemporary Worship Service Coming!" Did we know when or how? Absolutely not! We only knew that it seemed good to the Holy Spirit and to us, and so we announced it. Now remember, we have not messed with the two traditional services.

A new Worship Pastor to lead both the Traditional and Contemporary Worship teams was hired. He had a unique gift for leading both a traditional choir and a worship band. Together we worked to start the first little band and launched our first contemporary worship service on the first Sunday of September in 1997, exactly one year from my first Sunday at Grace. We had worked hard for several months to let members of the congregation and members of the community know that something new would be happening at Grace that Sunday morning. The night before the first service, one of our leaders called to ask me how many chairs to set up. I said, "100." He asked me, "Where's your faith, Pastor?" I responded "Okay, 110!"

Work to be contextual in music. If you are leading a contemporary service, use the best relevant, contemporary music.

The next morning, I arrived at church early to pray over the sanctuary and the fellowship hall. I was alone in the fellowship hall praying over the ugly orange chairs, and my eyes filled with tears. Just then a woman stuck her head in the door and said, "Pastor, this will never work." I tenderly responded, "I hope you're wrong." After greeting people at the end of the 8:30 service, I made my way into the fellowship hall to a standing-room-only crowd. I was stunned when 261 people showed up the first Sunday! By the grace of God, we had tapped into the heart language of our community. This "new style" of worship opened a portal into the unchurched community in our corner of southwest Florida.

For worship to effective, it needs to be contextual. When I was in seminary, one of my professors put it simply. "When you go fishing for fish, you put on the hook what fish like, not what you like." Lost people are too precious for us to waste time and energy trying to protect forms and styles of worship that do not open up the hearts and minds of people who are far from God.

If I served a church in a retirement community, we would do the very best worship music to engage lost 60-to-90-year-olds. If that was big band or swing music, then so be it. If I lived in a rural community and we had to do country and western music to reach people, then we would. Context is essential.

Excellent Worship

When I first arrived at Grace Church, we had two half-empty traditional worship services, but some of my biggest concerns in those early days were about what our members and guests experienced before they entered the worship service. The Friendship Court, a gathering area before you entered our narthex was a dark, dingy room with a river-rock floor that had big chunks of it missing. The walls were white with black shoe marks on them. Scattered throughout the room were old silk plants, broken-down umbrellas, and boxes of old church materials. The bathrooms were a dirty, vintage 1970's style, and worst of all was the condition of the infant and toddler rooms. The flooring was dirty brown industrial carpet. I'm not sure when it had last been cleaned. This was the "welcoming" space for my new church. Now remember, my first day in Cape Coral, we've got $29.16 in the checking account, and we owe 1.2 million dollars on the sanctuary.

As I looked around at our Friendship Court and infant and toddler rooms, I knew we had some sprucing up to do! So the chair of the Board of Trustees and I recruited a handful of guys to do some work. Together we threw away the worn-out silk plants and other junk, and we bought a five-gallon bucket of paint and painted the walls. The truth is that I started to paint, and the team asked to me to go back to my office and "write a sermon or something" because I was getting more paint on the floor and myself than the walls.

Next, I approached a saintly elderly woman in the church who had told me that she loved to give to special projects. I asked her for $1000 for new carpet in the infant and toddler rooms. Instead she gave me $2000 that allowed us to recarpet the floors and run the carpet halfway up the walls. We got thick padding to make the hard concrete safe for babies and bought new equipment as well. The bathrooms, though still looking 1970s, cleaned up well with some bleach and a scrub brush.

Hospitality matters, especially for first-time guests. You really do have only one shot at a first impression. Clean bathrooms, safe spaces for babies, and a welcoming environment go a long way at making a good first impression.

If you use projection, work as a team to achieve the best multimedia possible for your worship experience.

Remember when I mentioned the first contemporary service back in September 1997. We had a small band (guitar, drums, and keyboard with 3 singers), and we projected the words off an overhead projector onto a screen with a rip in it that we duct-taped together. Here's my point. Excellence is doing the best with what you have, not what you don't have. We could not afford video projectors in those days. We later added a second overhead project and screen, and that was progress. Excellence is a sliding scale. Do the best with what you have and slowly become more excellent.

Even today, our equipment is good, but not the "top shelf" stuff. In our largest, fullest venue we do not use image magnification, though we should. But we cannot afford to do it well. Until then, our screens will have images, words, and videos on them and that's all.

On several occasions, Cheryl and I have been blessed to travel to England. We have visited many of the great houses of worship—Westminster Abbey, St. Paul's Cathedral, York minster, and Lincoln Cathedral. We've visited and worshiped at Wesley Chapel, the church in London where John Wesley is buried.

As we spent our time at these great houses of worship, I thought again about the whole issue of worship. Once places of worship, these buildings were now no more than museums and concert halls. For the most part, vital Christianity was non-existent. Pastors have become curators of beautiful buildings. Congregations have become tourists. And I asked myself, *Why? Why have these houses that once were centers of praise and prayer of their communities ceased to be that in any real way?*

Even as I asked that question, God asked me a question: "Why is it that you do not worship me like you have in the past? Why is your life not a spring of praise and prayer to me?" My heart has the potential to become a barren place with only the forms of a once-vital and exciting worship life. An inviting physical environment for worship is important, but by itself it cannot create or sustain authentic worship. The hearts and lives of women and men are the sacred space required for authentic worship of God.

God made you and me for worship.

Make a list of at least three things that could help free up time for sermon preparation. Choose two and decide how you will accomplish them by specific dates. Make at least one related call or send one e-mail today.

Change/improve something that will affect a visitor's first impression.

Research

What We've Learned from Highly Vital Congregations about Worship
Amy Valdez Barker

There is no short supply on worship research in the field of ministry. There are a multitude of preferences about worship, styles of worship, liturgies of worship, and theology of worship. It is nearly impossible to nail down exactly what draws all types of people to worship. The question that arises as we consider the Towers Watson's research becomes, "Does what happens in worship matter to the vitality of a congregation?"

Keep in mind, the process for identifying factors that appeared more often in highly vital congregations were factors that could have "objective, observable and measurable results."[6] Elements like whether or not a congregation has a traditional or contemporary service are objective. Your congregation either has it or doesn't have it. Whether or not pastors use lectionary, topical, or blended preaching is observable. You can ask pastors which approach they use for preaching, and they can objectively answer with one of these responses.

1. Towers Watson's research states that, "High vital churches tend to provide a mix of both traditional and contemporary services."[7] The margin of difference between high vital and low vital congregations is 19 percent, which is slightly higher than the difference between congregations offering contemporary services only and high vitality. What is interesting to note, is that this dual-worship option is only significantly statistically beneficial for congregations with an average worship attendance of 350+. And offering both traditional and contemporary worship is statistically adverse for smaller and very small congregations. This signals to interpreters that there must be a critical mass present in order for two types of worship to be offered, and beneficial for health and growth in the congregation.

But do churches grow because they have more worship services, or do they grow first and then need to add additional services? Unfortunately, there is no definitive answer to that question, but controlling for size suggests that congregations tend to add worship services to accommodate additional attendees and to encourage growth."[8]

2. The next element that Towers Watson offers is the make-up of preaching in high vital churches versus low vital churches. Again, the margin between congregations that are considered high vital and the low vital is 15 percent. High vital congregations tend to have more topical preaching

versus lectionary-based preaching in traditional services. And pastors who were rated as effective in high vital congregations were said to have the leadership attribute of being "Inspiring through preaching."[9] Congregations that have worship described as "inspirational" also are more likely to be growing.

3. The last two elements of worship that were identified in high vital congregations have to do with contemporary services, which we already know are contextual to size in congregations, according to the TW research. Therefore, these findings are likely skewed toward medium and large congregations. These high vital congregations offer contemporary music during their contemporary services. They are also more likely to have multimedia resources available and used during their contemporary services. FACT data differentiates this element in congregations. They state that congregations that describe the character of their worship as "joyful, innovative, and inspirational," are more likely to experience congregational growth. The bottom line is that worship should be excellent, contextual, and relevant, no matter what the size of your congregation may be.

Worship

What is the most important strategic idea I have learned or thought about differently in this section?

_____

_____

What three things will I intentionally work on in the next six months?

1._____

2._____

3._____

Who can partner with me and what will be the time line for first steps on these three ideas?

                            Partnering with: **By When:**

1._____

2._____

3._____

What is the one thing that I can do today that will create new energy in this part of my ministry?

_____

_____

What from this section gives me hope?

_____

What do I want to share with my team, colleagues or mentors?

_____

_____

4.

The Power of Small Groups

They spent their time learning from the apostles,
and they were like family to each other.
They also broke bread and prayed together.
Acts 2:42, CEV

Highly vital congregations have small groups that build Christian community.

My wife Cheryl and I spent a week on vacation in northern California. While there, we visited a redwood forest. The redwoods are huge. Known for their enormous height and beauty as well as long life, the secret to the strength of these giant trees can be traced to their extensive root systems. Towering up to 350 feet, the redwood's root system is surprisingly shallow, no deeper than 6 to 12 feet. The physics of the tree wouldn't seem to work. The towering trunk and the shallow roots make for a disaster. They should just topple over!

So how do these giants stay upright? How do they keep from falling over? Here's the secret. Each tree, weighing in at nearly 500 tons, has roots intertwined with the roots of other redwood trees. This root system provides the stability that enables these ancient landmarks to stand for many hundreds of years. Seldom, if ever, will you find a redwood by itself; and if you do, it won't be standing for long. With a lifespan of up to 2000 years, the success and longevity of this kingly tree is a direct result of the tapestry of interwoven roots that connect with other redwoods. When strong winds and rain push against the giant trees, their interconnectedness keeps them upright.

The same thing is true for followers of Jesus. When we stand alone, our "root system" is not typically strong enough to withstand the winds and rains of life, but when we are "locked together," we can withstand almost everything.

You see this profoundly illustrated in the book of Acts. These first followers of Jesus endured and overcame the winds and rain of intense persecution and prevailed because the Holy Spirit fueled them for devoted community.

Think about it in this way. God exists in a community: Father, Son, and Holy Spirit. In the first creation story, God created Adam and Eve to live in community, saying that "it is not good for the man to be alone" (Genesis 2:18, NLT). When God called Abram, God also called Sarai and their family to begin a new nation, and they did it in community. King David had Jonathan and his "mighty men." Together in community, these men forged a new nation. The first thing Jesus did when he began his public ministry was form a team of 12 disciples. For three years these men lived together richly and deeply in community. It should be no surprise, then, that when God made you and God made me, God made us for community.

One of the things that break my heart as a pastor is watching people try to live the Christian life alone. I've met a lot of "freelance" and "free agent" Christians who move from place to place and who never have one church community to call home. Maybe they watch a television program or even watch a service online, but they never really engage and know other people. They can even sit in a sanctuary week after week, month after month, and year after year and never really connect to anyone. And when wind and rain comes, they fall. Every precious Christ-follower was made for devoted community.

A Devoted Community

Why do Christ-followers need to be a part of a devoted community? First, *a devoted community fuels our spiritual growth*. In just the New Testament, the phrase "one another" is found more than 60 times. Over and over, God gives Christ-followers a command to live together, and God does it for our good and our growth. This means that I will not grow as a follower of Jesus if I'm not connected to an "other."

This being connected to one another is illustrated beautifully among the first followers of Jesus. Let's look at the spiritual growth that took place.

> The believers devoted themselves to the apostles' teaching, to the community, to their shared meals, and to their prayers. A sense of awe came over everyone. God performed many wonders and signs through the apostles. All the believers were united and shared everything. They would sell pieces of property and possessions and distribute the proceeds to everyone who needed them. Every day, they met together in the temple and ate in their homes. They shared food with gladness and simplicity. They praised God and demonstrated

God's goodness to everyone. The Lord added daily to the community those who were being saved. (Acts 2:42-47)

A key word here is *devoted*. They made a covenant to be together. They never had to worry if someone was going to show up or not. A covenant is an agreement made in a moment of strength that carries us through the temptations of weakness. There are times when it's inconvenient to attend church, show up at a ministry team, attend a small-group meeting, or go to serve. When the temptation to skip comes, a covenant gets us there anyway. The disciples grew spiritually because of their devotion to one another, to teaching, fellowship, and worship.

As they took time for these things, something amazing happened. The Bible says that "a deep sense of awe came over them all." There was fuel in being together! Something amazing, something divine, took place in their gatherings. We can have deep times of communion and connection with God when we are alone with God. Those are impor-

All of us are created for community.

tant. As a matter of fact, they are essential. But moments of awe and wonder more often than not happen when we gather with a community of other Christ-followers. All of us are created for community.

Maybe you are old enough to remember when movies first became available to rent on video at home. There was a deep concern in Hollywood that this would cripple the movie theater industry. After all, the reasoning went, would anybody go to the movies theater when you could rent a movie to view at home for $3. What happened was the complete opposite: Theater attendance actually went up! ! An analysis of this trend showed that the reason it went up was because what happened in a theater full of people didn't happen in the living room around a TV. The smell of the popcorn, the surround sound, the laughing, screaming, and crying together was an environment that no living room could recreate.

Another example is the explosion in coffee shops. Do we go just for the expensive coffee? Or do we like being with other people, like being a "regular" who is recognized by the employees as well as other customers? We want to be known.

The first followers of Jesus experienced a community of faith together more vivid than any High Def, IMAX, 3-D movie watched alone. The missing fuel for many Christ-followers spiritual growth is not a just a crowd, but the awe that comes when the Holy Spirit unites us. The result among the first followers of Jesus was that they grew spiritually. They had in mind the common good over their personal gain. They were generous with their resources and experienced joy together.

Here's the second reason Christ-followers should live in devoted community. *A devoted community fuels our ministry.* The growth of the early church meant they had to solve the challenges that naturally followed. Remember, they had grown from a few dozen to several thousand people in a short amount of

---

Small Groups Invite People into Community   Chancey Green,
Building Better Moms leader, St. Andrew UMC,Frisco, Texas

Small Groups are a portal to the congregation connecting with people who might not otherwise engage the church.

Is your church fishing for people? In 2003, I moved to Kansas City and was invited to attend a Building Better Moms (BBM) meeting at The United Methodist Church of the Resurrection. At the time, I would have considered myself a nominally religious person and was not even necessarily searching for a church home. I joined the group and naturally began to grow in my faith and eventually joined the church. In 2011, I moved to Frisco, Texas, and was invited to a start-up church by a friend. I met with the pastor and spoke, with perhaps a little too much passion, of my Building Better Moms experience. He asked me to start up a group. Coming from a congregation of more than 16,000, I wasn't sure we could even fill a group (our church meets in an elementary school on Sundays and has no meeting space), but I saw the excitement in his eyes and knew I couldn't say no. A year later, BBM Frisco has launched with 54 members (only 8 of which are currently affiliated with our church).

Elden Cowley, pastor of the new congregation in Frisco, Texas, (St. Andrew UMC Frisco) is enthusiastic about the program. " I am extremely thankful for Building Better Moms (BBM). We are consistently looking for new and practical ways to engage and connect to new people in our community. BBM has shown itself to be an excellent way for women in our church and the greater community to connect with each other. I strongly recommend it to any church wanting to grow and meet people outside of its walls." In Matthew 4:19, it says Jesus called out to them, "Come, follow me, ...and I'll show you how to fish for people." Perhaps BBM, or something of the like, is the bait you need on your hook to fish for people?

---

time and with no organizational chart. One of the first problems the Jewish Christians had to solve together was that the widows among them needed food. A dispute broke out between two groups, those who spoke Aramaic (closely related to Hebrew) and those who spoke Greek.

This alone gives me peace, to know that the real first church had problems just like we do today. The Greek-speaking widows were being left out of the food distribution. The community needed a new ministry team to oversee the food distribution and break through the division of God's people.

> The community presented these seven to the apostles, who prayed and laid their hands on them. God's word continued to grow. The number of disciples in Jerusalem increased significantly. Even a large group of priests embraced the faith. (Acts 6:6-7)

Notice that there were seven on this new ministry team. The Holy Spirit fuels ministry done in community. Remember that every Christian is a minister. But we don't minister alone. The best, most fruitful ministry is done in teams of people united in purpose who use a variety of gifts and abilities to God's glory. This team of seven was so effective that "God's word continued to grow." Together, they were able to break through barriers and further the mission of Jesus.

This leads me to the last reason why Christ-followers need devoted community. *A devoted community fuels our transformation.* Clearly, the central person of the book of Acts is Paul, who was called Saul before he encountered Jesus. Remember that Saul was the zealot who wanted to stop the Jesus movement by persecution. He orchestrated the capture, imprisonment, torture, and even murder of many of the first followers of Jesus. And isn't it just like to God to choose this guy to not only become radically transformed by Jesus, but then become the chief missionary to spread the movement of Jesus to the world?

We might think Saul's transformation was simple, neat, and clean, but it wasn't. Like all of our transformations, it was messy. No one would believe that Saul, who once was a killer of the church, was now a pillar of the church. God used a man named Ananias to help the early church trust what God had done in Saul. Ananias lived in Damascus, and God spoke to him in a vision telling him to go and lay hands on Saul who was temporarily blind because of his encounter with Jesus. Ananias said (my interpretation), "Say what, Jesus! Don't you know this guy kills people like us?" The Lord was firm. "Do it, Ananias!" And as we read the rest of the story in Acts 9:17-22, we learn that Ananias obeyed.

What if Ananias had said no to Jesus? Without the help of Ananias and another brother, Barnabas, there would have been no Paul. This community of men was the instrument God used to complete the life transformation of Paul.

One of my favorite days of the year is Good Friday, when we hold an immersion baptism service at Celebrate Recovery. We use an old horse trough to baptize anywhere from 10 to 20 freshly redeemed men and women from all ages and stages of life. Each person's testimony is read as they stand in the horse trough. Each person is also surrounded by their devoted community of fellow Christ-followers who have supported them in their life transformation through Jesus. Tears flow as stories of life transformations are read. Shouts of "Hallelujah" and whispers of "Amen" fill the sanctuary.

After each person is baptized, the team of friends lays their hands on the soaking wet convert, and the pastor asks the Holy Spirit to seal what has just been done. It's a spectacular night that reminds us all what's at stake in being and doing Church.

Many of us grew up singing "We Are the Church," in which we proclaimed that the church isn't a building but that "we are the church together!"[1]

It's true!

TURBO-CHARGING OUR WESLEYAN TRADITION

John Wesley was a systems genius, whether he knew it not. There were other more eloquent preachers than John Wesley in his day. They could draw bigger crowds, but they could not seem to make the gospel "stick" to those who came to listen to them. Not so of John Wesley and the first Methodists. They were masters at ordering or systematizing seekers, new believers, and seasoned saints into groupings with the expressed purpose of growing in Christ.

Many people's perception of John Wesley is that he was a heroic, solo leader who rode into town on horseback alone, entering to stand in front of the coal miners with his Bible in hand to preach the Gospel. This would make a great movie, but it would also be wrong. Nobody traveled by himself or herself alone in the 18th century in England. There were bandits who beat and robbed people, so people traveled in groups.

Not only was traveling in groups a matter of physical safety for John Wesley and the early Methodists, it was a matter of spiritual and ministry security. Wesley knew he could not walk with God alone and do God's bidding alone. He needed a team! So he built one. According to Michael Henderson, "Wesley was no 'prima donna'; he was always a team player, and he modeled for his colleagues a collaborative style of directing and decision making."[2] In *Should We Change Our Game Plan?* George Hunter notes:

> Wesley traveled with a team; the major exceptions were when the team swelled to an entourage. As they traveled, Wesley did contextual training, and they reported and reflected upon what they had experienced in ministry in the town they just left; some of this insight found its way into Wesley's Journal.

When Wesley preached to a crowd, the invitation that followed was not to become a Christian on the spot, though people were welcome to do so. The invitation was to join to a Methodist Class Meeting that night. Wesley and his team started 1 to 5 groups each night. In these groups people discovered their faith and were held accountable to do good, avoid evil, and avail themselves of the means of grace. I believe that the road to recovery of Methodism in the 21st century is the recovery of joyous teams!

Roots keep a Christ-follower connected to Christ. Wings release a Christ-follower to serve Christ.

Wesley modeled small group and team ministry by forming them himself and then by replicating this small group/team ministry throughout the whole system of Methodist societies, class meetings, and bands. He understood that these small groups gave potential Christ-followers as well as Christ-followers both roots and wings. Roots keep a Christ-follower connected to Christ. Wings are what release a Christ-follower to serve Christ. Both were found in the early Methodist system of small groups.

In 1996, I was 36 and it was my first day as a lead pastor. Back then, a few more than 300 people gathered in one service. Back then resources were thin. We were thin on money, thin on staff, thin on programs. . . . I was even thin back then! They were tough days. But the miracle that is Grace Church today is a direct result of two things. First and foremost, the amazing grace of God. God has recklessly poured his unmerited favor into our church. But second, it was an amazing faith-filled, small group of Christ-followers who trusted God to do a new thing at Grace Church and in Southwest Florida. That core group claimed their calling to be ministers.

At one of my first gatherings with leaders, we were sitting in the fellowship hall around tables. I asked this small group of ministry leaders, about ten in number, to share their hopes, dreams, and visions for Grace Church. The chair of our personnel committee said, "I dream of the day when there are so many people coming to Grace Church that we have to hire a police officer to let people in and out at the corner of Hancock Bridge Parkway and Southeast 21st Place!" Some of us snickered. Others of us said "Amen!" Two years later, he was our first Director of Operations, and guess what? He hired the first police officer to let the hundreds of cars in and out of our property! That devoted community of leaders dreamed together of a community of followers of Jesus who would gather for worship and leave for mission. It was those few brave women and men in whom God placed a big dream for a community-shaping and world-shaking church. This is the potential power of a small group.

ON THE ROAD TO VITALITY!

I became a follower of Jesus through a parachurch ministry at my high school in Orlando, Florida. The area director of the ministry, John Zilen, took a liking to a bunch of pagan high school students, and he loved us into the Kingdom. Because I was not raised in the church, I did not know a thing about being a Christ-follower. Christian community, intimacy with God, and living a life of service were entirely foreign to me.

In this ministry, I was invited to be in a small group with a handful of other high school students. In that group, I said, "Yes" to Jesus and did what Sam Shoemaker said anyone could do. I gave as much of myself as I could to as much of God as I understood. I did not understand much about God, but one night in January of 1978, sitting on the gold shag carpet of my parents' home, I asked Jesus to come into my life. *My conversion happened in a small group.*

Then John and several other leaders began to mentor me in the faith. They invited me to begin studying the Bible. They gave me these clever little workbooks with Bible verses and questions for me to answer. They challenged me to memorize Bible verses and to learn to share my faith with my family and friends. In these groups, they taught me to pray and challenged me to serve. *My discipleship happened in a small group.*

Later after joining Pine Castle United Methodist Church, I joined a college-age ministry where my spiritual transformation continued. In those groups, I began to hear other college students who were wrestling with God about their "calling." Something began to stir in me, and I listened to them. Was God calling me to be a pastor? *My call to ministry happened in a small group.*

The list goes on and on of the good things God has done in my life within the gift of community. For the past thirty-five years, small groups have been that "incubator" where God has molded, shaped, broken, restored, healed, challenged, and comforted me. And it remains true today. Almost everything good that is happening in my spiritual life is connected to small groups.

Why Are Small Groups So Powerful?

I grew up on sitcoms. From *M.A.S.H.* to *Family Ties,* many an evening was spent laughing along with the crazy antics of these TV shows. *Cheers* was one of my favorite shows. The theme song, "Where Everybody Knows My Name," captures the hunger of the human heart to live in rich, deep community. This place of community where everyone knows your name is not just what we all want it's what we all need.

When a church gets beyond about 50 people or so, it is too big for everybody to know everybody. But we should never be too big for *everybody* to know *somebody.* The reason small groups are so important is that everybody has a deep desire to be known. I don't want people to just know my name. I want a few people to know my nickname. I want someone to pray for my aging parents by name when they are sick, and that can happen only in a small group.

> *Small groups have power. Offer as many varied, high-quality groups as you can.*

Recently, I got one of those letters that pastors hate to get. A woman sent me a scathing letter because she had been absent from our church for two years, and no one had contacted her. During that time, she had gotten ill, been in the hospital, and returned home to recuperate. In fact, I do know her name, but I did not "catch" that she was absent. Here's what I also know. Sadly, she had not connected with any small group in the life of our church. She had not invested the relational capital into any of the hundreds of groups we have, and nobody knew she was gone. Yes, it speaks to our need to have better systems that help us notice when someone is gone, but it also speaks to her unwillingness to join in any of the hundreds of community groups in our church. In a small group, there isn't a guarantee that a person will not drop out of church, but you will know when it happens.

As wonderful as our Friday night and Sunday morning gatherings for worship are, real community is not everybody sitting in long rows facing a pudgy Puerto Rican pastor (that would be me). Large gatherings of people for corporate worship and teaching are important, but it isn't Christian community. Real community doesn't happen in rows of chairs, but in circles. Real community happens when people sit eyeball-to-eyeball, knee-to-knee. When I can see you cry, we are in community.

Four Types of Small Groups

For decades as a Christ-follower and a leader in the church, I assumed that the primary purpose of small groups was discipleship or study. I now question this assumption. I believe that the primary purpose of small groups is community. Yes, Bible study is important, but Bible study alone is hollow if there isn't genuine, authentic, life-giving community.

At Grace Church, we have four primary types of small groups.

- Discipleship/study small groups
- Support/Recovery small groups
- Ministry teams
- Administrative teams

It may surprise you that we include ministry and administrative teams among our essential small-group communities. However, if, as I now believe, the most important purpose of a small group is developing relationships and that the task of the group comes second, then this broader understanding of small groups makes sense.

I believe the primary purpose of small groups is to create community.

Discipleship or study small groups are typically affinity-based groups of 6-to-12 people who meet weekly. In our context, these groups meet in homes, restaurants, or church. They are couples' groups, men's groups, and women's groups. The study materials in these groups vary from using a curriculum, a book, or just the Bible, depending on the need of the group or the expertise of the group leader.

Throughout the year, one of our staff puts together a "Deep Dive" one-page small groups guide for every sermon. They are available on the Sunday morning the message is given. Several times a year, usually during Lent and Advent, we encourage all our small groups to study the same material that we are preaching on. One year during Lent, we preached the Adam Hamilton material *24 Hours That Changed the World*. We sold the devotional guides, used the DVD studies in small groups, and preached the messages. We even started several short-term small groups for the seven weeks. This "campaign" emphasis bore great spiritual growth in our congregation at all four campuses.

We also offer dozens of short-term discipleship small groups throughout the year on almost every day and night of the week. The two ongoing classes we offer are our four-week new-member class called "Making My Connections" and our five-week spiritual gifts class called "Wired." Beyond these two core classes, a host of short-term classes on the Bible, marriage, parenting, recovery, and finances are offered.

Involving children and youth in small groups has been a part of our vision and strategy at Grace Church since the very beginning. At our middle and high school weekly gatherings, times of food, recreation, Bible study, and worship always include same-gender small groups for intimate sharing and care. Trained adults lead these groups.

In our children's ministry, Grace Kids, every Sunday children in the first through fifth grades gather in same-gender, grade-level small groups with a shepherd who is charged with guiding children in sharing responses to the lesson and prayer concerns. Our special-needs children's ministry (Through the Roof) allows these children to be integrated into small groups as a specially trained mentor sits with and assists each child in his or her small group.

Children and youth groups are critical— the more the better.

These discipleship/study small groups are the core groups in our church. When we first came to Grace, my wife Cheryl and I started two small groups. She started a Monday night women's group, and I started a Tuesday morning men's group. Sixteen years later, these two groups are still going. I do believe that leaders have to model what they expect. People will duplicate what they see their leaders do.

Support or recovery groups are the second kind of small group we have. Divorce Care and Grief Share are examples of short-term support groups at Grace Church. Ads have been placed in free local newspapers and on websites. In our most recent Divorce Care class 80 percent of the attendees are completely unchurched, and we have seen one person already become a follower of Jesus and join our church.

Celebrate Recovery has two kinds of small groups. At our Friday night Celebrate Recovery, after large group, our attendees are invited to attend ongoing men's and women's issue-based small groups. These are really "ports of entry" into deeper, more serious recovery groups. Every Tuesday night, we offer step study small groups that are gender specific and spend at least twelve months going through each of the Twelve Steps in a much slower and more intimate environment.

Our third kind of small groups are **ministry teams**. Do you think of your ushers as a ministry team? Or do they simply show up 30 minutes before the service and hand out bulletins? For years this was how we viewed our usher team, but more recently we have shifted and now work more intentionally at creating community teams. Again, when one of our usher's granddads is sick, someone needs to be praying and checking on their friend.

Creating a culture of community within a ministry is more art than science. Ministry teams are task-focused by nature. Our GED Team teaches GED. Our Community Garden Team plants and nurtures plants. The Worship Team practices and leads worship. Getting these teams to live in community is ongoing, never-ending work.

One of the tools we use to help us in this community-creating job is creating covenants.

Pastor Wes Olds is the campus pastor of the Cape Coral campus and the Grace Community Center. He is charged with leading our largest campus as well as an outreach center with more than forty vital ministries (In 2011 we assisted more than 26,000 of our neighbors in Southwest Florida). He is also a systems "monster." He knows how they work and don't work.

The final kind of small groups we have at Grace Church is **administrative teams**. These are the legislative groups that *The Book of Discipline of the United Methodist Church* says a congregation in our denomination has to have. More recently, *The Book of Discipline* gives congregations the latitude to order themselves administratively around their mission.

> Primary Tasks—The local church shall be organized so that it can pursue the primary task and mission in the context of its own community–reaching out and receiving with joy all who will respond, encouraging people in their relationship with God and inviting them to commitment to God's love in Jesus Christ; providing opportunities for them to seek strengthening and growth in spiritual formation; and supporting them to live lovingly and justly in the power of the Holy Spirit as faithful disciples. (Section VI. Organization and Administration, Para. 243)

We have been through our own legislative teams' metamorphosis for the past seven years. Currently, we have one "global" team that oversees all four campuses called the "Grace Leadership Council" made up of the Lead Pastor, the Campus Pastors, and several gifted laypersons with expertise and experience in leading large, complex organizations. Then each of the campuses has a "Guide Team" made up of the Campus Pastor and a team of gifted and representational leaders from that campus. These teams are charged with oversight, accountability, and policy setting. They carry the finance, personnel, and trustee responsibility for each campus.

The forms our teams take is less important than the way these administrative teams function. Their job is not the "adaptive" work of an operational (staff) team. They are legislative in nature. Every leader knows the frustration of having legislative teams trying to do operational work and vice versa. So the Trustees (a legislative team) are approving the vacation Bible school curriculum (adaptive work) or the staff (an operational team) is making decisions about starting a building campaign (legislative work). Getting clear about which team does which kind of work is essential if everyone is going to stay in their lanes.

We begin by spending significant time creating a holy environment for our meeting. Typical administrative meetings begin with what I call "the nod to God" at the beginning. This is usually when the paid religious person (the pastor) says the perfunctory prayer invoking God's presence and guidance. Now I believe God hears even perfunctory prayers, but do they change us? Most of the time, the answer is no. In my experience God is not the center of the conversation in administrative meetings. God's will is not the focus of the meeting, but rather personal agendas and preferences of the people on the committee.

That is why after reviewing the covenant, by reading and reflecting on it out loud, we share "glory sightings." Glory sightings are just that . . . sightings of God's glory! Where in our lives inside and outside the church have we seen God at work? This alone changes the tenor of an administrative meeting. Then we move to prayer concerns and prayers. Praying for a team member whose unmarried daughter is pregnant or whose spouse has cancer takes time. In a typical two-hour administrative meeting, this kind of holy work can take an hour or even more.

Then we move to learning together. Teams need to be constantly stretched and challenged in their leadership understanding and experience. Watching a leadership DVD, reviewing a chapter in a book, or simply reviewing our church vision, values, and strategy are ways in which as a team can learn together.

> *Only after we have loved God and one another well are we ready to do the work of the church.*

Only after we have loved God and one another well, and have been stretched and challenged as leaders learning together are we ready to do the administrative work of the church. We have found that there is more unity when making important congregational decisions if this environment is intentionally set.

When they are honest, many pastors and church leaders admit that they despise at worse and tolerate at best administrative meetings. Seldom do I hear a pastor say, "I cannot wait to get to church tonight for the Finance Committee meeting." The truth is many of these meeting are either perfunctory or blood-baths. Yet the administrative oversight of the work of God's people who are joining Jesus in his mission is some of the most important work on planet Earth. Leaders get to create the environment for these meetings, and they must do them well. There is too much at stake.

When finances are not raised, managed, and spent well; when staff is not hired, deployed, evaluated, compensated, and even fired well; when facilities are not designed, built, updated, and maintained well, the Kingdom of God suffers. These administrative tasks are holy work just like preaching, marrying, burying, and baptizing!

Small Group and Team Covenants

We have discovered that a covenant helps every small group and team at Grace Church that builds one function better. Assumptions about expectations go away when a team does the work to create a covenant together. Buy-in is high when everyone is invited to participate. Conflict resolution is figured out before the fight! Exit strategies are talked about before they are needed. Everyone on the team wins with a covenant.

Leaders of vital churches figure out ways to create a constellation of small groups where seekers, new Christ-followers, struggling saints, and long-time believers can live richly and deeply in community.

Now let me be forthright. With four campuses, I cannot honestly say that every ministry team has a covenant. We are working on it, and remember what I said earlier. It's more art than science. And it takes constant diligence to not just build covenant communities but to maintain them.

Leaders of vital churches figure out ways to create a constellation of small groups where seekers, new Christ-followers, struggling saints, and long-time believers can live richly and deeply in community. They know that every person who calls their church their spiritual home needs to be in a small group where everyone knows their nickname and can pray for their sick grandma. Now, that's church!

Small Group and Team Covenants

The creation of a covenant can help any Grace Church small group or ministry team enjoy healthy and holy relationships as we work together for God's glory.

We Put the "Fun" in Dysfunction!

If you haven't noticed by now, life is a contact sport. Not a day goes by that we are not bumping into one another's ideas, egos, or spirit. Patrick Lencioni's best-selling book, The Five Dysfunctions of a Team *reveals the problems people have in the corporate world as they try to work together. These dysfunctions are:*

- *Absence of trust*
- *Fear of conflict*
- *Avoidance of accountability*
- *Lack of commitment*
- *Inattention to results*

Now, let's be honest. The church is not immune to these dysfunctions! Some of the worst conflicts can happen in church meetings ... or worse, in the parking lot after the meeting! We are like porcupines gathered together in a snowstorm: We need each other to keep warm, but we can be prickly.

There is Hope!

The creation of a team covenant can help overcome these dysfunctions by providing a foundation of trust. Remember, covenants are God's idea! Just as covenants can anchor our faith in God, they can also protect our relationships with one another. Writing down the actions that will build trust between people enables the team to thrive and work in a healthy environment.

How To Build A Team Covenant

It is crucial to have everyone that is on the team participate in coming up with a covenant that makes sense to the group. These simple questions can get people talking about the behaviors that build trust. As people respond, record their answers on a white board or poster.

*1. Who is the **greatest leader** you have ever been around? Why?*

*2. What is the **greatest team** you've ever been on and what made it great?*

*3. What would make **this group** a great team?*

Once you have your list, take the answers and prepare 6-8 statements that are important to the team. Some things to include are agreements about
- *The primary purpose of the team*
- *How conflicts will be handled (Matthew 18:15 is a start!)*
- *When is it okay to be absent? (Sick, out of town...)*
- *How often we will pray for one another?*

A Sample Team Covenant

Our Team Covenant:
1. We seek to be faithful to God's Vision for Grace Church: "To partner with God in transforming people from unbelievers to fully devoted disciples of Jesus to the glory of God!"
2. We seek to offer Grace Church a united team agreed upon in honest discussions where we listen to one another, disagree agreeably, keep discussions confidential, and have each other's back.
3. We seek to make our meetings a priority by attending unless we are sick or out of town. If we have to miss, we will communicate our absence to the chairperson. If we don't hear from someone, we will call and make sure they are okay.
4. We will meet the second Monday of the month at 7 p.m.
5. We will pray for each other once each week.
6. We will handle any potential conflicts in a biblical way. We will start conversations with questions and seek to understand one another's perspectives. The Bible (Matthew 18) serves as our guide on resolving conflicts.

What to Do with the Covenant

The covenant needs to be agreed upon by everyone on the team and any changes made together. Read the covenant at the start of each meeting and ask: "How are we doing at keeping our covenant? Is there anything we need to say to one another to build trust as a team?" Remember, the covenant is first and foremost a "mirror" for each team member to examine his or her own heart and commitment.

Wes Olds Campus Pastor,
Cape Coral Campus and Grace Community Center

Adapted from "Team Covenant," posted March 2012 on MyCom.htm/UMCom.org. Used by permission of United Methodist Communications, The United Methodist Church.

Quick Victories

Begin and lead a Discipleship/Study or Support/Recovery small group.

Commit to writing a covenant with one of your ministry or administrative teams, using the "Small Group and Team Covenants" as a guide.

Research

What We've Learned from Highly Vital Congregations about Small Groups

Amy Valdez Barker

Remembering that Towers Watson used indicators of vitality that were *descriptive, differentiating, quantifiable, and available*[3] helps leadership understand the focus of the research. It also tells us what data our denomination has not been collecting. The old adage says, "What gets counted gets attention." It's important to remember that this element of the research is not exhaustive, but only descriptive and limited by what was available at the time of the research.

The CTA Report states that "Small groups include study, fellowship, and service; programs include classes and other activities."[4] This description leaves a lot to interpretation of the data and of leaders using the data. Therefore, we will use several sources to invite leaders of the church to consider what small group ministry means for their congregation in relation to the research reported.

The reality is that today, small groups in congregations can take on a variety of shapes, sizes, meaning, and direction. Small groups include study, fellowship, and service; programs include classes and other activites. What Towers Watson identified is that the number of small groups reported makes a difference to the impact on vitality. In this element of the research, there is no negative impact for congregations of differing sizes. In fact, even in very small churches, the high-vital congregations had one more small group than the low-vital congregations.[5]

1. **The number of small groups affects overall vitality in all three factors: Attendance, Growth, Engagement.** TW reported that 60 percent of churches with high vitality have more than 5 small groups. They also shared the gap between highly vital large congregations and low-vital large congregations is at 66 percent. In other words the churches identified with high vitality with an average worship attendance of 350+ have 15 more small groups on average than the same size congregation identified as low vital. The number of small groups in a congregation matters.

The critique on this data is that it does not clearly identify the size composition of the small groups, nor the actual activities conducted in these small groups (with the exception of the study, fellowship, and service definition).

2. **Regardless of size, more vital churches have more programs for**

children (under 12 years old).[6] The gap between high-vital and low-vital churches in this element is no less than 34 percent. Even in very small congregations, the high-vital churches have at least two more programs for children than low-vital churches. In large congregations the gap is astronomical. Churches identified as high-vital have 149 percent more programs for children than the low-vital congregations. The type of programs offered for children have not been identified in this research; however, it does clearly indicate that in high-vital churches, children matter and the programming the church offers points to how they value their children in these congregations.

3. **Regardless of size, more vital churches have more programs for youth (12-18 years old).**[7] The same differentiations between programs for children are identified in programs for youth. The greatest gap exists in larger congregations identified as high-vital and low-vital congregations. They have 84 percent more programs for youth than their low-vital counterparts. Again, this signals to leadership that youth ministry ought to matter no matter what size congregation you serve.

Small Groups

What is the most important strategic idea I have learned or thought about differently in this section?

_____

_____

What three things will I intentionally work on in the next six months?
1._____
2._____
3._____

Who can partner with me and what will be the time line for first steps on these three ideas?

Partnering with: **By When:**
1._____
2._____
3._____

What is the one thing that I can do today that will create new energy in this part of my ministry?

_____

_____

What from this section gives me hope?

_____

What do I want to share with my team, colleagues or mentors?

_____

_____

5.

Reaching Across the Street and Around the World

*I assure you that whoever believes in me will do the works
that I do. They will do even greater works than these
because I am going to the Father.*
John 14:12

Highly vital congregations strategically implement outreach and mission that is local and global.

These are haunting and intimidating words for any serious follower of Jesus. I know they have haunted me. It doesn't take too deep a look into any one of the four biographies of Jesus to see some pretty amazing stuff. He walked on water, raised dead people to life, and fed thousands with a boy's sack lunch. Jesus cast out demons and quieted storms with a word. And we are going to do greater things than this? What did Jesus mean?

Now mind you, I believe in miracles, and I believe that they still happen today. By God's grace, I have seen cancer unexplainably disappear. These power moments though are rare, and even the most gifted healer can't replicate the healing power of Jesus. Nobody quite measures up, but Jesus did say, "The person who trusts me will do not only what I'm doing but even greater things" *(author paraphrase)*.

So what gives? Is it our lack of faith? Do we just not trust God enough? I think we misunderstand the mission of Jesus. Here's an important question for us to wrestle with: Why did Jesus come to earth? Was it to demonstrate the power of God? I don't think so. I think that Jesus came to this sin-sick, war-torn, blue-green planet not to flex God's muscles but to show God's heart. Jesus did not come primarily to demonstrate God's power but rather to show us God's love! Every miracle, every demonstration of power that Jesus exercised was motivated by love.

Why did Jesus raise Jairus' daughter from the dead? It was to demonstrate the Father's love for all his children. Why did he feed the hungry crowd of 5000 men plus all the women and children? It was to show God's heart that loves to provide for his kids. Jesus' manifestations of power were for a greater goal: to show God's love!

The "greater things" Jesus invites us to participate in are about demonstrating, illustrating, and expressing God's love to people. These are the greater things that we are invited by Jesus to do. Demonstrating God's love is the primary task of followers of Jesus. It also is why the local church exists.

One of the best biblical illustrations of this is found in Luke 10, the well-known parable of the Good Samaritan. The context within which Jesus tells the story is important.

> A legal expert stood up to test Jesus. "Teacher," he said, "what must I do to gain eternal life?" Jesus replied, "What is written in the Law? How do you interpret it?" He responded, *"You must love the Lord your God with all your heart, with all your being, with all your strength, and with all your mind, and love your neighbor as yourself."* Jesus said to him, "You have answered correctly. Do this and you will live." But the legal expert wanted to prove that he was right, so he said to Jesus, "And who is my neighbor?" *(Luke 10:25-29)*

The person to whom Jesus tells the parable is a religious, church-going fellow. He has an honorable question for the Master. "What should I do to inherit eternal life?" Jesus does what he so often does. He answers a question with a question. "What does the Torah, the law of Moses say?" Like a good student of the Torah, the questioning man answers, "Love God with all that you are. Love your neighbor as you love yourself" (Deuteronomy 6:5; Leviticus 19:18). This was Hebrew 101!

Then comes this final word. "The legal expert wanted to prove that he was right, so he said to Jesus 'And who is my neighbor?' " What was the man trying to justify? He was trying to insist to Jesus that indeed he loved God completely and loved his neighbors as he loved himself. The question was a bit of a ruse. "And who is my neighbor?" was the man's self-justification. "I'm a good guy! I go to church. I tithe. I'm in a small group." But in the end, the man was setting himself up for Jesus to firmly push into his heart.

Jesus replied, "A man went down from Jerusalem to Jericho. He encountered thieves, who stripped him naked, beat him up, and left him near death. Now it just so happened that a priest was also going down the same road. When he saw the injured man, he crossed over to the other side of the road and went on his way. Likewise, a Levite came by that spot, saw the injured man, and crossed over to the other side of the road and went on his way. A Samaritan, who was on a journey, came to where the man was. But when he saw him, he was moved with compassion. (Luke 10:30-33)

To the listening crowd, Jesus' story is fine at first. A Jewish traveler being beaten and left for dead by bandits was sad but not uncommon in that day. Traveling alone made this a real possibility. The priest and the Levite (temple assistant) did not stop to help the brother out. Jesus doesn't tell us why, but perhaps their reasons would be the same as ours. They were busy, in a hurry, and figured someone else could help the man. It was when the man who *did* stop to help the Jewish traveler was introduced that the crowd would have begun to murmur.

The Jews despised Samaritans. There would have been boos and hisses at this point in the story. Samaritans were half-breeds from the other side of the tracks. There was a long-standing feud between Jews and Samaritans. This was way beyond the passion we experience between rival football teams. It was more like the hatred that long existed between Protestants and Catholics in Northern Ireland. And yet, the Samaritan had compassion for the man. He was a good neighbor. And what he does next modeled for that religious man in the first century and for religious men and women in the twenty-first century what it means to really love our neighbor.

How does the local church love her neighbors? That's the bottom line in this story of Jesus. It's about demonstrating God's love. St. Francis of Assisi said, "Preach the Gospel at all times and if necessary, use words." This Samaritan preaches the Gospel, but how?

How Do We Love Our Neighbors?

First, *we love our neighbors by giving immediate aid.* The compassionate Samaritan in Jesus' story finds the man beaten and battered on the road. What does he do first? After a bit of rudimentary EMT work, he loads the battered man up on a first-century ambulance, a donkey, and takes him to an inn, a place to heal. The Samaritan stops the bleeding! This was his first expression of loving his neighbor.

Second, *we love our neighbors by giving ongoing advancement.* The Samaritan gets the man's bleeding stopped and get's him settled in a room. Was his responsibility for loving his neighbor as he loved himself over? No. The Samaritan healer not only stops the bleeding but makes a commitment to the man's complete healing. He agrees to pay all the man's bills, however much that might be. He wants to help the man move from dependence to independence. This is what I call advancement.

Third, *we love our neighbors by our continual advocacy.* Jesus' story has ended, but he turns to the religious man and asks one more piercing question. "What do you think? Which one of these three was a neighbor to the man who encountered thieves? "Then the legal expert said, 'The one who demonstrated mercy toward him' " (Luke 10:36-37).

Jesus lifts up the hated and despised Samaritan as the hero of the parable. He gives a voice to a voiceless man. He puts on a pedestal for all to see one who is least likely to be considered a neighbor in the Jewish crowd he is addressing. "This guy," Jesus says, "gets noticed by God." Jesus advocated for people on the margins.

Aid, advancement, and advocacy. This is what it meant in the first century and what it means in the twenty-first century to love our neighbors. Mother Teresa says it so well.

It is not enough for us to say: "I love God," but I also have to love my neighbor. St. John says that you are a liar if you say you love God and you don't love your neighbor. How can you love God whom you do not see, if you do not love your neighbor whom you see, whom you touch, with whom you live? And so it is very important for us to realize that love, to be true, has to hurt. I must be willing to give whatever it takes not to harm other people and, in fact, to do good to them. This requires that I be willing to give until it hurts. Otherwise, there is not true love in me and I bring injustice, not peace, to those around me. It hurt Jesus to love us. We have been created in His image for greater things, to love and to be loved.[1]

Mother Teresa is right! We have been created in God's image for greater things. Jesus ended his story with this charge, not only to us individually but to the local church, "Go and do likewise."

TURBO-CHARGING OUR WESLEYAN TRADITION

You have nothing to do but to save souls. Therefore spend and be spent in this work. And go always, not only to those that want you, but to those that want you most.

Observe: It is not your business to preach so many times, and to take care of this or that society; but to save as many souls as you can; to bring as many sinners as you possibly can to repentance and with all your power to build them up in that holiness without which they cannot see the Lord.

John Wesley[2]

There is no doubt that the early Methodists were passionate evangelists. They had a passion to reach the unchurched (those with no spiritual heritage), de-churched (those with a lapsed spiritual heritage), and the over-churched (those with a wooden spiritual heritage).

But John Wesley described the nature of salvation carefully. He did not hold to evangelism as simply rescuing people from eternal damnation. Salvation was not just a heavenly issue. He understood that salvation was also an earthly one.

By Salvation I mean, not barely, according to the vulgar notion, deliverance from hell, or going to heaven; but a present deliverance from sin, a restoration of the soul to its primitive health, its original purity; a recovery of the divine nature; the renewal of our souls after the image of God, in righteousness and true holiness, in justice, mercy and truth.[3]

Jesus did not come only to save us from the hell we are heading to, but also to save us from the hell we are living in! For Methodists, salvation is both a heavenly and an earthly enterprise.

The first Methodists wove together this theological understanding by expecting Methodists to do not only "works of piety" (personal holiness) but also "works of mercy" (social holiness)—both of these fused together put a Christian on the path to perfection in love. This was part of the genius of Wesley and the early Methodists. As Steve Harper notes, "There simply is no one way, or better way, to make Christ known. On the contrary, we must search for those places and ways where the Holy Spirit has preceded us to create "ports of entry" for the Gospel and the temporal and eternal benefits it brings."[4]

Some early Methodist "ports of entry" were field preaching, literacy efforts, medical ministries, homes for orphans and widows, opposing slavery, and micro-loans for the poor. John Wesley *preferred* to minister to and with the poor.

It is well a few of the rich and noble are called. O, that God would in-crease their number! But I should rejoice (were it the will of God) if it were done by the ministry of others. If I might choose, I should still (as I have done hitherto) preach the gospel to the poor.[5]

The "target audience" of the Methodist movement was the people on the margins of society. When Wesley writes to a wealthy woman who was a Methodist Society member, he could be speaking directly to most of us.

Do not confine your conversation to gentle and elegant people. I should like this as well as you do. But I cannot discover a precedent for it in the life

---

Reaching Out

Lori Shannon, Certified Lay Minister, Gray UMC, Gray, Iowa

Declining church invites unchurched families through outreach dinners, parties for children, campus outreach and family events.

Gray United Methodist Church in Gray, Iowa, had been in decline for some time, even though it marked its 125th year in 2011. With dwindling attendance, no children in church, and the building badly in need of up-dates, the future looked bleak. In the last two years, however, the church has taken steps to reinvent itself. With new unchurched families with chil-dren moving into town, the church has hosted two outreach meals, gather-ings such as back-to-school and Halloween parties for the children in the area, and a community Thanksgiving meal. Future plans include a possible after-school Sunday school for children and encouraging the unchurched children to participate in the church's Christmas program. In addition to these plans, the church has undertaken several new ministries including support of a minister doing campus outreach The church also hosted its first four-church service in the community rose garden involving local churches and pastors with plans to make this an annual event. Cosmetic improvements have been made to the church as well. A paint facelift inside and out, new carpet, and the church's first cross and flame give it a more welcoming appearance. A person not attending the church but living in town commented, "Finally there's some life in that church!"

of our Lord, or any of his Apostles. My dear friend, let you and I walk as he walked. . . I want you to converse more, abundantly more, with the poorest of the people, who, if they have not taste, have souls, which you may forward on their way to heaven. And they have (many of them) faith, and the love of God in a larger measure than any persons I know. Creep in among these, in spite of dirt, and a hundred disgusting circumstances; and thus put off the gentlewoman.[6]

As I mentioned in an earlier chapter, the system for evangelism and discipleship of the early Methodists was very purposeful. United Societies, Class Meetings, and Bands each had unique emphases to help people grow in Christ. A lesser-known group was a part of the first Methodists. They were the "penitent bands." *In John Wesley's Class Meeting,* D. Michael Henderson explains the need for this special group.

This final group of Wesley's system was specifically designed for those who lacked the will power or personal discipline to live up to the behavioral demands of the class meeting but still had a desire to overcome personal problems. Since the target population of the Methodist system was what many considered 'the dregs of English society,' the instructional hierarchy of groups needed some alternative route for those with serious social dysfunctions. The primary goal of the penitent band was to restore its members to the mainstream of society and its regular channels of growth.[7]

The penitent bands met on Saturday nights, designed to keep them out their "old haunts." The minister in charge was assigned the responsibility to help them deal with their problems, especially alcoholism. The group was rigorous in format and stringent in means of personal reform; similar to today's Alcoholics Anonymous.

It was not only the poor that early Methodists sought to reach, but addicts as well. Those on the margins of society became the focus of the Methodist movement.

ON THE ROAD TO VITALITY

So what might it look like for a 21st century, culturally relevant church to weave together and hold in tension a ministry with "works of piety" and "works of mercy?" How might The United Methodist Church resist a great divorce between personal and social holiness? For the past 16 years, we have been experimenting with living in this tension. As a result, we have seen our works of piety and our works mercy come together to transform individuals, families, and increasingly our community.

Local Outreach and Mission

One of Grace Church's stated goals is to lower the crime rate in our community. I think you would agree that that is a God-sized goal. Though difficult to measure with any certainty, we believe we are accomplishing the goal. When a single Mom comes to Grace Community Center, gets her GED and then her nursing degree, she can support her family and no longer has to sell her body on the street. When a drug addict becomes a follower of Jesus through one of our Recovery Ministries, gets clean and sober, then he stops stealing to support his habit.

How do we join Jesus in accomplishing such dramatic transformations? Many of our efforts contribute to the effort, but our work is largely organized into two ministry areas, Grace Community Center and our Recovery ministries.

Grace Community Center

In 2007, Grace Church took a big leap of faith when we purchased an old stand-alone grocery store with the goal of opening a community center. The 57,000 square foot store on 8.5 acres had been sitting empty for several years. We wanted to create a holistic ministry center. We dreamed of a place for a food bank and a thrift store. We hoped to offer ministries like an after-school drop-in ministry for high school students to help lower after-school crime and reach at-risk students for Christ. We anticipated having ministries for the homeless, the aged, and those with AIDS. We had visions of offering haircuts, pet food, and a community garden.

By late 2008, after struggling with permit and zoning issues and a build-out of 23,000 square feet, the Grace Community Center opened. Today all of these dreams and hopes plus more are a reality. And here's the best part! Every one of these ministries opens doors for spiritual conversations. In 2011, 278 people became followers of Jesus through the Grace Community Center ministries. Extending aid and offering advancement became portals for the Spirit of God to transform lives.

Take time to train volunteers for both global and local mission work.

The Community Center is open seven days a week with some kind of ministry going on. Wes Olds is the Campus Pastor who oversees both the Cape

Coral campus and the Grace Community Center. We have a full-time manager of the Thrift Store and several part-time staff. It takes hundreds of volunteers each month to stay open.

Once a month on Saturday mornings (we call it a Third Saturday outreach) and twice a month on Wednesday evenings, we have outreach events. The core ministry is the food pantry. Our guests are warmly welcomed. Worship music is playing while snacks are offered. Spread throughout the room are tables offering other services like GED, medical screenings, cooking classes, AIDS testing, mammograms, haircuts, pet food, and more.

Guests are sent to intake booths where a host welcomes them, gets their vital information, and someone from our prayer team simply asks, "Is there anything we can pray for you about?" Because we believe in prevenient grace, we know God has already been at work in that person's life. We are just joining Jesus. Again and again, week after week, the Holy Spirit opens portals into people's souls. Seldom does one of these outreach days go by without five to ten people becoming followers of Jesus.

Does this outreach sound expensive? It is! We still owe *millions* of dollars on the Grace Community Center building. It was a financially risky initiative from the beginning, and it still is. Every mortgage payment we make is a relief, a blessing, and a prayer answered. This isn't our ministry; it's God's ministry. We could never do it on our own.

Training Volunteers

As we have done this kind of holistic ministry with people on the margins of our community, we have learned the importance of training. When we send a short-term mission team to an international site, the team spends six months in training. One day we had an epiphany of sorts. "We'll spend six months training six people to go 10,000 miles for two weeks, but we don't train hundreds of people we send around the corner every week!" We immediately developed a local "send" ministry orientation.

In this simple, one-hour orientation, we walk children, youth, and adults through our Grace Church vision, values, and strategy. We want our unpaid servants to know how what they are doing at the Grace Community Center connects to the broader church ministry. Then we challenge the servants to live by Rueben Job's *Three Simple Rules*. Do no harm, do good, and stay in love with God. These rules are easily understood and profoundly livable.

Several months back, I stuck my head into one of the orientations before an outreach event. The room was packed with new servants. What caught my attention was a band of older elementary-aged girls. Only later did I get the rest of the story. Cameron is a sixth grader who has grown up at Grace Church. For her eleventh birthday, she asked her mom if she could have a sleepover on a Friday night with six of her friends so that on Saturday they could help at the Grace Community Center. Her birthday gift was serving the poor and marginalized! I wept when I heard this story. That's Church!

Global Outreach and Ministry

By all practical measures, if you were to evaluate our ministry at Grace Church in 2001, we would have graded out pretty well. In most areas of our ministry at Grace, things were on the increase. God's sovereign favor had been given to our church. In the five plus years of my ministry at the time, God had been very good to us as a church and to me as a pastor.

I had been seduced into a "Jerusalem-only ministry."

So, what was the problem? The problem was that as a pastor, I had been seduced into a "Jerusalem-only ministry." Remember the words of Jesus in Acts 1:8?

"But you will receive power when the Holy Spirit comes on you; and you will be my witnesses in Jerusalem, and in all Judea and Samaria, and to the ends of the earth" (NIV).

In seminary, I learned that Jesus was using expanding concentric geographic areas to illustrate our calling to the entire world. I believed this scripture, I just didn't practice it much.

I heard a term to describe Christ-followers who confess faith in Jesus, but do not reflect that confession with their lives. The term is "practical atheists." Belief never makes it into everyday life. When it came to Acts 1:8, that was me. If you asked me if I believed in an "Acts 1:8" personal and corporate lifestyle, you would have gotten a resounding "Yes!" But, did I actually live it out in my personal life and leadership as a pastor? That was a harder question to answer.

I had been involved in missions. As a ten-year youth ministry veteran, I had led teams of youth to Appalachia, urban centers in America, the delta of Mississippi, Puerto Rico, Mexico, and Costa Rica. Missions were a core value of our church. As a Wesleyan, I was committed to John Wesley's maxim "The world is my parish." Grace Church had an expanding ministry to the poor, homeless, and addicted of our community. But was missions the mission of my life and my ministry? Not really!

All of that changed in one week. One of our leaders had been to a Global Focus Conference in Georgia and returned to Grace Church on fire. And soon, her fire spread. For months, we planned a Global Focus week at Grace Church. At our Wednesday night, New Community service, we would invite Dan Betzer, Senior Pastor at First Assembly of God in Fort Myers. He is a giant in world missions. Then on Friday night and Saturday morning, Dick McLain and his team from the Mission Society for United Methodists (now The Mission Society) would lead many core leaders from Grace Church through a seminar on becoming a globally-focused church. Sunday morning, Dick McLain would preach. Missionaries from Japan would meet with as many small groups as possible during the week. As we planned this week, I never could have imagined the change that would occur in our church and me.

My personal defining moment came on Saturday at the Global Focus seminar. I'm still not sure what did it, but it was probably the video, *The Harvest,* that closed the seminar. It broke me. Dick had asked me to close the seminar with prayer. When I stood to pray, my heart was beating so hard, I thought it would come out of my chest. After several minutes of silence, I asked our people to join me at the altar to pray. With tears running down my face, the Holy Spirit gently convicted me of my leadership sin of omission. The Spirit revealed to me that as a pastor I had been seduced into a Jerusalem-only ministry. It was not intentional, but it was the truth. In my zeal to reach the lost of Cape Coral and the surrounding area, I had forgotten about the rest of the world.

I asked God for forgiveness that Saturday. I told God that if he would give me another chance, I would do all I could with his help to lead Grace Church to be a globally-focused church. Did I know all that this means? Absolutely not, but isn't that the delight of being a leader in the church? I was scared to death. This changed everything . . . how we spend our money, the buildings we build, the priorities we make, the staff we hire and more.

I'm still red-hot to reach my Jerusalem. With God's help, that will never change. God has just expanded my vision and the vision of Grace Church to partner with him in reaching the millions of people who have no access to the gospel. This means no church in their village, no Bible in their language, and no Christ-follower in their life.

Practically, this has meant developing a team that leads what we call our "Send Global" ministries. At each of our campuses, it is non-negotiable for that campus to have at least one global mission partner. This team oversees our strategy that invites Christ-followers who call Grace Church their spiritual home to "give, go and pray" as they join Jesus in his mission. Giving allows us to financially support our ten global mission partners in places like India, Ghana, Costa Rica, and Nicaragua. Going means we send 15 to 20 short-term mission teams to these countries for mission projects. Praying invites our people to pray weekly for a mission partner as well as join a prayer team that prays "back home" when short-term teams are serving in another country.

One of the tools we use to inform and inspire our people to join Jesus in his global mission is to hold an annual Missions Conference in the winter. We invite several of our global partners to join us for the week. They are invited to our small groups, children's and youth ministries, and are involved in worship services. During this week, we challenge our people to "give, go and pray." We also invite our people to consider full- time missionary service.

When we send out a short-term mission team, we commission them on a Sunday morning. The mission is explained, and the team members kneel at the altar while hands are laid on them. Prayer cards with a picture and names of the team members are printed and given to our congregation. This gives greater ownership of our short-term mission teams to the entire congregation.

As I reread Acts 1:8 recently, I noticed how Jesus used the word "and." He said, *"You will be my witnesses in Jerusalem, and in all Judea and Samaria, and to the ends of the earth"* (NIV). Jesus never said, "Reach your Jerusalem first, then go to Judea, Samaria, and the rest of the world." I think Jesus meant for us to have a biblically balanced church with a passion and a strategy to reach lost people in our backyard and around the world.

Recovery Ministries

While every United Methodist congregation shares certain DNA, and as the Towers Watson research has revealed, every vital congregation has several key shared behaviors, every congregation is also unique. At Grace Church, we have claimed the blessing and the identity of having many fruitful recovery ministries.

I believe Jesus is rallying his troops but giving us a very different charge. Jesus tells us, "At my signal, unleash heaven!"

I love the movie *Gladiator*. Maximus is the Roman general who leads the Roman army to victory over the barbarians. In the opening scene of *Gladiator*, Maximus rallies the troops for battle. He mounts his horse and turns to one of his officers and says, "At my signal, unleash hell!" Then he rides to a gathering of other officers and gives them a final word of encouragement where he ends with the statement, "What we do in life echoes in eternity!"

I believe Jesus is rallying his troops but giving us a very different charge.

Jesus tells us, "At my signal, unleash heaven!" His dream is for the realities of heaven to become the realities of earth. He invites those who follow Jesus to take the Jesus movement to the people and places most in need of his grace. But Jesus also reminds us, "What you do in this life echoes in eternity." We have but one life to live. Will we spend our lives and be spent making earth look more like heaven?

This is why I am so passionate about recovery ministries. Better than anything I have found, it makes the realities of heaven the realities of earth. Let me illustrate. Kim came to see me about eleven years ago. Her husband Jim was drinking a fifth of vodka a day. He would wash it down with a twelve-pack of beer and a fist full of Vicodin. To top it off, Jim had a girl friend on the side. Kim was a codependent spouse who enabled Jim to live this unhealthy and unholy lifestyle. I told her to get to our Celebrate Recovery on Friday nights and make her way to the women's codependency group. And she did.

On Father's Day, Jim came to church mostly because Kim begged him to. Hung over, Jim listened to my message on being a God-honoring father. At the end, I invited all the men to come to the front to pray. Jim stumbled to the front. He left church and that very week, Jim got sick and tired of being sick and tired. He ended up in a rehab center.

Flash-forward ahead with me today. Jim and Kim are married and lead our marriage ministry. He is a passionate evangelist who loves and lives to help connect people to Jesus. He and I have preached at churches in India together. Jim is a transformed man. This is why I love recovery ministry. It unleashes heaven into men and women like Jim and Kim.

A recovery ministry that transforms lives is not about slick programming, heroic personnel, or state-of-the-art properties. You can buy a boxed set and get the nuts and bolts to start a recovery ministry in your church, and it can (and likely will) fail. It's not about the mechanics.

About one in three people who come to Grace Church have self-identified as being a person in recovery. On a typical week, in our thirteen weekly worship services at three campuses, we will have four Celebrate Recovery services with about 400 adults, youth, and children. Of the remaining nine worship services, there are about 2000-2100 people in attendance. Note two things with me. First, our ratio of people attending recovery ministries is extremely high. About one-fifth our total weekly worship attendance comes from recovery ministries. But secondly and more importantly, a disproportionate number of our first-time commitments to Jesus come from our recovery ministries. We are convinced it is because of some underlying (often unspoken) principles that are at the core of who we are. They are deeply embedded in the organism of Grace Church. They are strands in our DNA. These are theological and philosophical assumptions that make our recovery ministries at Grace Church flourish and bear "much fruit, fruit that lasts."

Four Principles of Recovery Ministry

First, *everybody has an "it!" Jesus came to deliver people from the hell they are living in as well as the hell they are heading to.* Even though everybody has an *it,* not everybody knows they have an *it.* Trust me, everybody around the person knows they have **it**! If you don't know what your *it* is, ask those closest to you and they will tell you (if they believe you really want to know). You can deny *it.* Try to forget *it.* Try to drink, drug, shop, sex, or sleep *it* away, but *it* remains.

The Bible calls this "it" reality in every human being "sin." Sin is anything that keeps me from being the person God made me to be. Any attitude or action that keeps me from being the woman or man God made me to be is sin. And everyone is a sinner.

What does *everyone* mean? Everyone! No exceptions! No "special people." Everyone misses the mark. You might hit the bull's eye some of the time but not all of the time. And God's standard is perfection. It's a no-hitter every time. It's a hole-in-one every time. It's a perfect 300 game in bowling every time. Do you do it right every time? I thought not!

It's been more than thirty years since I have drunk alcohol. Seldom do I ever even think about drinking. By God's grace, one day at a time, I have remained sober, but here's the deal. I know that until I die, "it" is still in me. I never want to get to the place where I think I am beyond "it." I always want to be humbled by "it" in my life.

Do you know what your "it" is? God wants to show you. If you are a follower of Jesus, his Holy Spirit wants to reveal to you your "it." He loves you that much. This "it" message minimizes (though sadly does not eliminate) the us/them stuff. When the culture of your church acknowledges that everyone is messed up, that all God's children are dysfunctional, then the playing field is leveled. It creates a culture where people know it's safe to talk about their stuff.

A defining moment for our church was one Sunday morning when Bob stood at the pulpit of our church to share his testimony. He began with "Good morning. My name is Bob, and I'm a follower of Jesus in recovery from sexual addiction." You could feel the air get sucked out of the room. For the next twelve minutes, Bob appropriately shared his struggle and victory in Christ. When he finished, the place went crazy! They stood up and cheered. Yes, for Bob, but I believe mostly because someone finally had the courage to tell the truth in church! It created an atmosphere of grace were even the most difficult issues of life can be talked about with hope.

My brothers and sisters in ministry, please, please, please . . . if you want to do this ministry, learn to be appropriately vulnerable about your own hurts, habits, and hang ups. Name your "it." I am convinced that part of the reason God has blessed our ministry at Grace Church so much is that on my first Sunday, as I was preparing the congregation to receive communion, I said, "You take a piece of the bread and you dip it in the cup. We use grape juice and not alcohol, so if you struggle with alcohol like I do, please know that this is a safe table for you." When I speak at our recovery ministry, I say, "My name is Jorge, and I'm a follower of Jesus in recovery from drugs, alcohol, and control." Name your "it."

Friends, our church is only hearing half the gospel if all we talk about is the hell that we are going to be rescued from without talking about the hell we need rescuing from right now. Preach, teach, and live the full gospel!

Second, *resist spiritual malpractice. Spiritual malpractice is offering Jesus the Healer without the people, places, and processes for Jesus to heal.* 1 Corinthians 13, the love chapter, teaches us "the most excellent way" of love. Paul gives us that memorable litany about the nature of love that is at the heart of Christian community. When all is said and done, the brochures can be slick, the music can be memorable, the message can be polished, but without love at the heart of it all, it's empty. God's heart is for people.

Several years ago, I found myself looking at the church I was privileged to pastor and asking myself, "Are people at the heart of our ministry? Do we prioritize people over programs, personnel, and properties?" One way to answer this question for me has been to look at the number and quality of our healing ministries. Healing ministries are those ministries with the stated intent of helping people get well God's way.

> *Create ministries that help people allow the healing power of Jesus to work from skin deep to bone deep.*

It seems to me that many churches could be accused of spiritual malpractice. By that I mean, they offer people Jesus the Healer without offering healing ministries. They are faithful to the evangelistic call to know Jesus as the Forgiver, Healer, and Leader of their lives, but then stop short of helping that new relationship take root inside the battered life of the fledging Christ-follower.

Remember that Jesus' twelve disciples walked with him for three years, and they still didn't "get it" completely.

Here's the question: Does my church offer healing ministries that help people intentionally get well God's way? Can you point to a handful of ministries that help people allow the healing power of Jesus to work from skin deep to bone deep? Yes, some healing happens in Sunday school classes and other small groups, but I mean do you have ministries in your church that exist for the sole purpose of helping people heal up? Remember healing takes time and intentional work.

At Grace Church, we have been very intentional about creating safe places for people to get well God's way. These ministries by design help seekers, new Christ-followers, and seasoned saints connect in safe places with competent people with the expressed goal of getting well and whole, and staying that way. For us they include:

1. Celebrate Recovery
2. Celebrate Kids
3. Celebrate Teens
4. Step studies
5. *The Twelve Steps for Christians Bible* studies
6. Secular recovery (AA, NA, and SA)
7. Stephen Ministry
8. DivorceCare
9. GriefShare
10. Financial Peace University
11. Crown Ministry
12. Marriage Ministry[8]

These ministries create the safe people, places, and processes for Jesus to do his best work!

Third, *we are not only delivered from the addiction but in recovery from the damage. Recovery is a step-by-step spiritual growth process to move people from sin, self, and Satan to Christ-likeness.* Many of us were raised in an "I've been delivered" theology, and by this it meant, "I'm not an alcoholic anymore," or "Praise God, Jesus rescued me from my addiction!" Implied is that I won't ever struggle with this anymore. I still believe that God delivers me, but I have to qualify the statement with the harsh reality that the damage of sin in my life remains. Recovery addresses the damage.

I often ask a person who is new to faith in Jesus, "How long did it take you to mess up your life?" They will often respond with "Well, Jorge, I began drinking at eleven, and now I'm thirty-seven, so I'd say twenty-six years, give or take a year." My response is always the same. "Then how about giving Jesus at least as much time to fix your life as you gave to mess it up!" Remember that sin is progressive in our human experience. People don't just wake up one morning with their lives in a ditch.

Our recovery from sin is also progressive. What recovery does better than anything I have found in the church is break down the spiritual journey into twelve simple yet profound steps that help people remove the roadblocks in their relationship with God. We talk about sanctification a lot. Sanctification is that life-long process of becoming more and more like Jesus.

In Ephesians 3:14-21, Paul masterfully weaves together the presence of the Holy Spirit, the love of Jesus, and the power of our heavenly Father working in our lives. It evokes a life-long pilgrimage with God. It's our Triune God beckoning us...romancing us...wooing us to dance. It's Father, Son, and Holy Spirit, "God in three persons, blessed Trinity" calling out to us, "I have so much more for you!"

What this means practically for me as a leader is that I have to be patient with people as they journey in their recovery. I find myself thinking more like a missionary than a North American pastor. The "barbarians" we are reaching spill coffee in the sanctuary and don't take their kids out of church when they are losing their minds. So "Susan" finds Jesus on the floor of the strip club she was working at, dries her tears, and finishes her set. And "Tasha," a prostitute, who then found Jesus, kept turning tricks because it was all she knew. It took time for her to find the freedom in Christ that facilitated her going back to school and becoming a nurse. Judgment in this kind of ministry has to be reserved.

Have you ever seen those silly infomercials? They show you their amazing gizmo or the remarkable gadget, and then the announcer says, "But wait, there's more! You get two for $19.95!" Our relationship with God is kind of like that without all the hype. We start this journey with Jesus, and then God says, "But wait, there's more!" In January of 1978, I just wanted a reason to live, and God

Recovery ministry is messy, and it will wreck your church.

gave it to me. He reached out and touched an addicted high school senior. Then God said, "But wait, there's more I want to do in you." Two years later, God called me to be a pastor. "But wait, Jorge, there's more." He brought Cheryl, my greatest gift on earth, into my life. "But wait, there's more." And for thirty-two years, God has kept saying to me, "Wait, there's more that I want to do in and through you. I'm not finished with you yet." That is what God is saying to each of us. "But wait, there's more!" Recovery ministry invites Christ-followers to consistently hear the "more" call of God.

Fourth, *recovery ministry is messy, and it will wreck your church. But the joy of getting a front-row seat at life change is worth all the hassle.* At our tenth anniversary, we gathered the entire Grace Church family under a tent on our property to announce the purchase of the Grace Community Center. We asked 50 people who had been redeemed by Jesus through our ministry to stand and hold a placard that on one side gave a word or phrase about what their life was like before they knew Jesus and what it was like now that they knew Jesus. Even though I was a part of planning the morning, I never could have prepared myself for the impact. Person after person, young and old, stood holding up their signs and flipping them over. It wrecked me. As the worship band led us in a song of gratitude to God, my knees buckled and I fell to the asphalt with my arms extended to the sky in gratitude to our great God. This is the kind of wrecking that recovery ministry can do for you.

I love parties. And the Bible is clear that what makes heaven throw parties is when lost, hurting, broken, addicted, disenfranchised people make their way to Jesus. "In the same way, there is more joy in heaven over one lost sinner who repents and returns to God than over ninety-nine others who are righteous and haven't strayed away! (Luke 15:7, NLT).

Our God loves to party! So at Grace Church about four or five times a year, a bunch of grateful men and women in recovery gather together to party in one of our baptism celebrations. During these baptism celebrations, we will baptize 10-20 people. In the crowd will be mentally challenged children and adults. In the crowd will be Christ-followers in recovery from drugs and alcohol. In the crowd will be homeless people, middle-management staffers, and occasionally a six-figure executive. And it is a party. The best I've ever attended! It's my new addiction.

As I have said, when I came to Grace Church, we had about 330 people and $29.16 in the checking account my first Sunday. I was younger than most everyone in the building, but I had a prayer in my heart that I had been taught by a Southern Baptist minister. So I prayed, "Lord, send us the people nobody else wants." Ten years later, the Holy Spirit prompted me to add, "Lord, send us the people nobody else wants or sees." And here's the deal. God has, and it has wrecked my life, and I'll never be the same. Jesus is saying to you and me, "On my signal, unleash heaven, Church, because what you do in this life echoes in eternity."

Quick Victories

Canvas your congregation about local outreach ministries that they might begin. Invite their suggestions but also name specific types of ministries, such as food bank, clothes closet, GED, recovery ministry. Identify which areas get the greatest response, and build a team to design and implement the new outreach ministry.

Take an international short-term mission or a disaster relief trip with a handful of leaders from your church.

Research

What We've Learned from Highly Vital Congregations about Outreach and Mission

Amy Valdez Barker

Towers Watson's research did not give many clear indicators of outreach and mission. The primary reason was that the data was not available. This in and of itself signaled to church leadership a critical question about what has mattered to us as a denomination in the past

The key element to consider from this area of the research is that "service" was lumped under small groups. According to GCFA, the way the church collected data on missions was to count the number of participants in Volunteers in Mission each year. This was the only number collected. However, when Towers Watson did their interviews of congregations considered to be highly vital, they heard over and over again the value of mission in ministry for these congregations.

Works of mercy are clearly a part of our Wesleyan Heritage and a means of grace that we cannot deny or forget. The invitation to leadership becomes, "How will you invite and inspire the disciples in your congregation to serve God by serving neighbor?" Will it matter? In our Wesleyan tradition, we must respond with a resounding "YES!"

Outreach and Mission

What is the most important strategic idea I have learned or thought about differently in this section?

_____

_____

What three things will I intentionally work on in the next six months?

1._____

2._____

3._____

Who can partner with me and what will be the time line for first steps on these three ideas?

Partnering with: **By When:**

1._____

2._____

3._____

What is the one thing that I can do today that will create new energy in this part of my ministry?

_____

_____

What from this section gives me hope?

_____

What do I want to share with my team, colleagues or mentors?

_____

_____

Conclusion

CONGREGATIONAL VITALITY MEANS FRUITFULNESS

Several years ago, Pastor Wes Olds and I were in Costa Rica training about 40 Methodist pastors and leaders. One night there was an earthquake. Guess what? Pastor Wes and I slept through it! The excitement came and went, and we slept through it.

Sounds to me like a lot of local churches. The earthquake happened. Jesus came to earth...taught, healed, preached, died, rose again, and ascended. But the story did not end there. The Holy Spirit came at Pentecost and gave birth to the Jesus movement that in 2000 years has grown from 120 to more than two billion. Yet many of us have been sound asleep during the action.

Three Spiritual Realities

Recently, I began to think about how fruit grows. In that trip to Costa Rica, each morning at our hotel, we were served breakfast. It began with a plate full of fresh pineapple, mangoes, strawberries, and watermelon. Some farmers in Costa Rica carefully tended their gardens so that fresh fruit could be grown. There are certain characteristics that assure fruit production. Certain environments insure fruitfulness.

The same is true for local churches. I believe there are three spiritual realities that mirror agricultural realties that are present in highly vital local churches. As laity and pastors together create these healthy and holy environments, they will bear the fresh fruit of congregational vitality.

The first spiritual reality is: *Healthy fruit grows on vigorous plants.* Sick plants and trees do not bear fruit. It takes vigorous plants to grow healthy fruit. In Matthew 7:17-18 (NLT), Jesus uses this agricultural reality to teach a spiritual truth. "A good tree produces good fruit, and a bad tree produces bad fruit. A good tree can't produce bad fruit, and a bad tree can't produce good fruit."

We know this is an agricultural truth. An unhealthy tree will produce unhealthy fruit and vice versa. Growing up in Central Florida, we had citrus trees in our yard. Healthy trees produced luscious, juicy fruit; but diseased trees produced dried up fruit unfit for eating. The quality of the fruit that you see growing on the outside is a reflection of the nature of the tree.

This insight applies to congregations as well. The quality of the fruit that congregations produce is a reflection of the character of the congregation. Local churches were designed by God to make disciples of Jesus Christ for the transformation of the world. Sadly, far too many local churches make other things like programs, staff, or properties the main focus. This is not the Master's design. When a local church is vigorous, it grows fully devoted disciples of Jesus, and the community and world are the beneficiaries of this miracle of life transformation.

The second spiritual truth is: *Abundant fruit comes from cultivated plants.* Jesus was a wise teacher, and he used common, everyday illustrations from the life of first-century Israel to teach God's truth. Vineyards were as common in Jesus' day as boats are on the Florida beaches where I live. Listen to his teaching about vineyards in John 15:1-7 (NLT):

> I am the true grapevine, and my Father is the gardener. He cuts off every branch of mine that doesn't produce fruit, and he prunes the branches that do bear fruit so they will produce even more. You have already been pruned and purified by the message I have given you. Remain in me, and I will remain in you. For a branch cannot produce fruit if it is severed from the vine, and you cannot be fruitful unless you remain in me.
>
> Yes, I am the vine; you are the branches. Those who remain in me, and I in them, will produce much fruit. For apart from me you can do nothing. Anyone who does not remain in me is thrown away like a useless branch and withers. Such branches are gathered into a pile to be burned. But if you remain in me and my words remain in you, you may ask for anything you want, and it will be granted!

Jesus compares our corporate life with God to that of a vineyard being cared for by the gardener. The Father is the Gardener. Jesus is the vine. Christ-followers together are the branches that produce fruit. But where is the Holy Spirit? More than one Bible scholar has taught that the Holy Spirit is the unseen and unspoken sap that flows from Jesus to his followers. I really like that!

Now there is a ton of stuff in these verses about what it means to abide with Jesus, but I want to focus on just one part. It's in verses 2 and 3 where Jesus speaks of cutting off and pruning branches. Several years ago I read the book *The Secrets of the Vine* by Bruce Wilkinson. I thought for years that these verses meant that if my life was not fruitful God got rid of me, cut me off and somehow I lost my salvation. The problem was that I never read those two little words in the second sentence: "of mine" in this translation or "in me" in others. How can you be "in Jesus" and somehow be cast away from him? We have all been though seasons of fruitlessness and still remained in Christ.

To help clarify this Jesus goes on to say in verse 3: *You have already been pruned and purified by the message I have given you.* So here's the kind of person in Christ who Jesus is talking about in verses 2 and 3. They are fruitless, yet purified or clean. How does this work?

The word that is translated "cut off" in verse 2 is the Greek word *airo*, which can mean, "Lift up." It does not necessarily mean "cut off" or "takes away" as many translation have rendered it.. The image I see here is this. The gentle vinedresser leans over to a low-lying branch and lifts it up. Now, why? The answer is simple. It has to do with being clean.

New vine branches have a tendency to grow along the ground. They get dusty; and when it rains, they get muddy and mildewed. The branch becomes sick, useless, and fruitless. Are they cut off? No. The branch is too valuable for that. The vinedresser goes through the vineyard with a bucket of water looking for these sick branches. He lifts them up, washes them off, and ties them up to the trellis. Soon, the branch is thriving and fruitful. Now let me give a personal and a corporate application.

Personally, this is what God does to us when God disciplines us. Sin covers our lives. We want our own low-lying ways. We like our low-lying ways. Sometimes we secretly love our low-lying ways. Pretty soon we are sick and dying. The tender God we serve reaches down and lifts us up and cleanses us. The cleansing is God's divine discipline. And divine discipline is evidence of divine love! God cultivates Christ-followers so that we can be more fruitful. Just as diligent parents discipline their children out of love and because they want them to "grow up right," our Father disciplines us so that we will grow to be fully devoted disciples of Jesus.

I recalled distinctly a time when God used my father-in-law, John, to discipline me. Cheryl and I had had been married less than two years, and we had a brand new baby boy, Daniel Aaron. The day Cheryl returned home from delivering Daniel, all five of us (Cheryl, Daniel, John, Nancy, and I) were jammed into our little apartment. I was watching TV and asked Cheryl (mind you she had just given birth to our son) to fix me a sandwich! Writing it now even makes me sick to my stomach. Her mom jumped up and fixed me the sandwich, and I did not even have a clue as to how selfish and insensitive I had been. I was still in great need of recovery.

Later that day, John and I were outside when he in a most gentle way put his arms around me, recounted my being a jerk, and told me with great love, "Jorge, you are not being a very good husband." It cut deep, but it was very much needed. God used John to discipline me, and I took several small steps in my fruit-bearing that day. Abundant fruit comes from cultivated plants.

Corporately, God disciplines us as local churches in the same way. Having been a part of three local church turn-arounds while serving at Grace Church over the past sixteen years, I have noticed that the journey to be an inwardly focused church happens slowly. Churches become comfortable in their low-lying ways. Pretty soon, they are sick and dying. God in God's tenderness reaches down to prune us. Local churches that receive the tender discipline of God can bear much fruit. Local churches that refuse to be pruned die. Sometimes the pruning means making the painful decision to discontinue a dying worship service. It hurts when it gets cut off. Other times the pruning involves risking our understanding of what it means to be a church "family" in order to reach new, diverse kinds of people who are living in the neighborhood of our church. Pruning hurts, but it is for our good and our vitality.

The third spiritual reality is that *bountiful fruit is attractive!* For farmers nothing gets their blood flowing like a bountiful harvest. Orange growers love the sight of trees weighed down with ripe oranges ready for harvest, and nothing breaks their heart quite like unfruitful trees. Orange trees are supposed to produce oranges for eating and juicing.

Jesus ends his teaching on the fruitfulness of his followers in John 15 with this declaration in John 15:8 (NLT):

> *"When you produce much fruit, you are my true disciples. This brings great glory to my Father."*

Jesus is clear that fruit bearing is expected of his followers, and that this fruit brings glory to the Father and not to the fruit bearer. Remember that in this metaphor the Father is the Gardener. He is the Grower, and the fruitfulness of his vineyard brings him accolades, not the fruit. Can you see the humor here? Imagine the grapes taking credit for being lush. No! The fruitfulness of the vineyard says nothing about the branches or the fruit and everything about the Gardener! He gets the credit.

When the local church bears the fruit, God gets the credit! He gets the accolades. God gets the applause. God did the work. We were just available. When the lost are found, God is glorified. God did the seeking, searching, and finding. When the found are discipled, God is glorified. God did the cultivating, pruning, and harvesting. This healthy, abundant, bountiful fruit is *solo gloria dei* or "to the glory of God alone."

In the summer of 2005, my wife Cheryl and I were standing in the New Room in Bristol, England. We were serving as hosts for four other Florida United Methodist pastors and their spouses. The Florida Conference is blessed to have the Mr. and Mrs. B. W. Simpkins Wesley Study Retreat. The hope of the Simpkins family is that the retreat will spark the fire of Wesleyan revival in the hearts of Florida United Methodist clergy.

The New Room served the Wesleys and the early Methodist movement as a meetinghouse and preachers' overnight accommodations. A curator dressed in full attire gave us a first-person monologue from John Wesley about the use of this historic building. Following his speech, a time of questions and answers ensued. Remaining in first person, our curator politely answered our questions.

One of our clergy on the retreat asked, "Were these pews here during your time?" She was referring to the pews that were permanently affixed to the floor of the New Room. The curator responded "Oh no! In my time we used wooden chairs or benches so that after our services we could push them to the corners of the room and use it for a medical clinic or a food ministry." With these words, I began to softly weep. And there were two reasons for my tears.

The first reason I wept was very personal. Years before, I had led an initiative to have the pews removed from our traditional sanctuary and replaced with chairs, but not for the reason you might think. It had nothing to do with making our sanctuary less traditional, but rather the reality that we could seat another 125 people in the same amount of space with definable chairs. The change had the added bonus of creating more usable space for other ministries when the sanctuary wasn't being used for worship. In leading this initiative, I took a beating from a few of our members. Sitting in the back of the New Room, I felt validated for this painful leadership move, as I knew our church had moved to the center of our Wesleyan identity. The early Methodists valued people over decorum and ministry over respectability.

The second reason I wept was not so much a personal thing as it was a professional or ministry reason. I wept because of the distance the people called Methodist have drifted from our unique witness in the Christian communion. In my mind, these haunting words of John Wesley floated through my thoughts:

> *I am not afraid that the people called Methodists should ever cease to exist either in Europe or America. But I am afraid lest they should only exist as a dead sect, having the form of religion without the power. And this undoubtedly will be the case unless they hold fast both the doctrine, spirit, and discipline with which they first set out.*[1]

Something inside me knew that this simple metaphor of movable chairs was a part of the Wesleyan message and ministry that was missing from our church. My fear was and is that these words of John Wesley have become a reality in many places in our church.

Vigorous vitality is the hope and dream of God for every church in every place. There are conditions under which this kind of vitality is not only a possibility but a reality. God has done God's part. He has given us all that we need for our local churches to be vital: the Holy Spirit with his gifts and fruits, and ordinary people to be instruments of community and world transformation. Let's join Jesus in his mission!

I love the church! *Solo Gloria Dei!*

Appendix

OVERVIEW OF TOWERS WATSON
RESEARCH LEARNINGS
Amy Valdez Barker

The research findings in this book were discovered in a study conducted by Towers Watson, a leading global organization with expertise in research. The study was sponsored by The Call to Action Steering Team with the purpose of uncovering clear, data-supported, information about vital congregations, how they function and what brings different results for these congregations. Towers Watson looked for data that gave indicators of vitality that were *descriptive, differentiating, quantifiable, and available.*

The Call to Action Project: Our Adaptive Challenge

The Call to Action Steering Team was commissioned by the Council of Bishops and the Connectional Table to continue the work begun by the Call to Action project launched in 2009. The mandate was to: "seek an objective operational assessment of the Connection that will result in findings and recommendations leading to the re-ordering of the life of the Church for greater effectiveness in making disciples of Jesus Christ for the transformation of the world." The work had two areas of focus. The first area was to find a new way of uncovering information about vital congregations that was more data driven rather than opinion driven. This resulted in the Towers Watson Vital Congregations Research. The second focus was on the Institutional Structure, which became the APEX Assessment Report. Both reports led to the development of the "Adaptive Challenge" presented to the Council of Bishops and the Connectional Table of The United Methodist Church.

The Adaptive Challenge was to:

"Redirect the flow of attention, energy and resources to an intense concentration on fostering and sustaining an increase in the number of vital congregations effective in making disciples of Jesus Christ for the transformation of the world."[1]

TOWERS WATSON'S METHODOLOGY

Towers Watson is a reputable and trusted institution that has served organizations of all shapes and sizes. They introduced a new technique called data-mining, that looks deeply at the numbers already collected about our congregations. This method had never been used in the history of the UMC to evaluate the millions and millions of data-points generated by the year-end reports submitted by U.S. UM congregations each year. They set forth to answer a key question that had been brewing among leadership in the church, "how can we measure levels of vitality in statistically valid and reliable ways?"[2]

As they utilized the data-mining process and employed the statistical technique called regression-analysis to determine both the direction and magnitude of any identified relationships with the desired outcome, they discovered "drivers" that seemed to appear with more frequency amongst the highly-vital congregations demonstrating the desired outcome of attendance, growth, and engagement. The research opened up the door for the denomination to develop a methodology that would define the baseline fundamentals every congregation needs in order to be equipped for the best and most successful future towards health and vitality, God could offer them.

THE VITALITY INDEX: Which Congregations Are Most Vital?

To learn what is different about highly vital congregations, Towers Watson first had to identify which congregations were thriving above and beyond the norm of congregations in the UM congregations in the United States. Towers Watson identified the "vitality index" in order to mine the millions of data points turned in each year by these congregations.

Attendance, Growth, and Engagement

The primary factors used to numerically identify the norm of vital congregations were attendance, growth, and engagement. Within the three factors of attendance, growth, and engagement, they used several different ways to compare congregations across the United States. This information came from the Year-End Statistical Reports from the office of the General Council on Finance and Administration. The specific numbers for each factor of attendance, growth, and engagement are listed below. The variables had to work for small and large, urban and rural, new and established congregations. The variables often include comparison as a percentage of membership or percentage growth to help apply these evenly across congregations.

Attendance
Average worship attendance as percentage of membership
Number of children, youth, and young adults attending as a percentage of membership
Growth
Change in average worship attendance as percentage of membership over five years
Change in membership over five years
Change in annual giving per attendee over three years
Change in financial benevolence beyond the local church as a percentage of church budget over five years

Engagement
Professions of faith per member
Annual giving per attendee

Each church was then assigned a numeric rating of 3, 2, or 1 based upon these variables of growth, attendance, and engagement when compared to all other congregations across the United States. The sum of these numbers identified where each congregation landed on the scale of all U.S. UM congregations. They were then assigned a location based upon this continuum of vitality. Congregations with the number 3-5 were identified as LOW VITAL. Congregations with the number 7-6 were identified as MEDIUM VITAL. Congregations with the number 8-9 were identified as HIGH VITAL. (This meant that these High Vital congregations scored a "3" in two of the areas and at least a "2" in the third, meaning they were well balanced across the three areas.)

Finding the Highly Vital Congregations

After looking at the scores across the 32,228 congregations with available information, the research showed that 15% of the UMC churches were HIGH VITAL, 49% were MEDIUM VITAL and 36% were LOW VITAL. The 4,961 or 15% of congregations who scored as high-vital included very small and very large congregations from every possible church setting.[3]

The statistical technique that they used to calculate these measures is common to what is used in consumer, employee, and political research. More and more organizations are beginning to use data-based facts to guide their decisions.

The pastors, lay leaders, and staff of these 4,961 high-vital congregations were then surveyed to discover which of the 127 possible tested elements were most likely to be in these congregations to a greater degree than others. The research was looking for some behaviors that could be significantly more likely, in a statistical way, to be present in a highly vital congregation than in a medium or low vital congregation.

Learning from the Highly Vital Congregations

5,851 bishops, district superintendents, pastors, staff and lay leadership from the denomination responded to the survey. Of the respondents, 19% of the sample surveyed represented high-vital congregations. From these surveys, researchers discovered that sixteen elements or "drivers" grouped into four key areas were significantly more likely to be found in high-vital churches than in the medium and low vital congregations.

Pastoral Leadership

1) Pastors of highly vital congregations focus on developing, coaching and mentoring to enable laity leadership to improve performance.
2) Pastors of highly vital congregations influence the actions and behaviors of others to accomplish changes in the local church.
3) Pastors of highly vital congregations propel the local church to set and achieve significant goals through effective leadership.
4) Pastors of highly vital congregations inspire the congregation through their preaching.
5) Pastors of highly vital congregations show a contribution to vitality after three years, and 36% of the highly-vital churches have pastors who have served more than 10 years.

Laity Leadership

6) The lay leadership of highly vital congregations are effective.

7) The lay leadership of highly vital congregations demonstrate a vital personal faith.

8) The lay leadership of highly vital congregations rotate responsibilities.

9) Highly vital congregations have a greater share of membership who consider themselves leaders in the church (within the last 5 years).

Worship

10) High vital churches tend to provide a mix of both traditional and contemporary services (if the congregation worships more than 350 weekly).

11) Highly vital congregations tend to have more topical preaching versus lectionary-based preaching in their pulpits, in traditional services.

12) Highly vital congregations offer contemporary music during their contemporary services.

13) Highly vital congregations are more likely to have multi-media resources available and utilized during their contemporary services.

Small Groups

14) Highly vital congregations have more small groups than other congregations in their size category. Small groups affect attendance, growth, engagement and can include study, fellowship, support groups, and ministry teams.

15) Regardless of size highly vital congregations have more programs for children (under 12 years old).

16) Regardless of size, highly vital congregations have more programs for youth (12-18 years old).

Keep in mind it is the collection of all of these elements that affect vitality. Aiming towards having all of these factors will affect vitality in congregations and increase effectiveness.

For the full report with the list of all 127 drivers and a more detailed look at results, please visit www.umccalltoaction.org and visit the area titled "The Challenge," where you will find the full research reports.

Notes

Introduction

1. The "Grace Church Playbook" is a living document that defines our vision, values, strategy, structure, and theology. It describes why and how we do ministry, regardless of the context.
2. *Call to Action Steering Team Report*, 2010, p. 37. The complete report can be found at www.umccalltoaction.org/the-challenge.

1. Spiritual Pastoral Leadership

1. Jaime J. Stilson, *The Power of Ugly: A Celebration of Earthy Spirituality* (Woodinville, Wash., Harmon Press, 2010).
2. Scholars disagree on whether Paul was directly or indirectly the source of First and Second Timothy and Titus. Since all agree that these letters are related to Paul in some way, the importance and meaning of the letters is not in question.
3. *Call to Action Steering Team Report*, 2012, p. 15.
4. James Harnish, How to correct someone who works for you. wwwfaithandleadership.com/blog/03-23-2010.
5. John Wesley to John Trembath, August 17, 1760, in *Letters of John Wesley*, Telford Edition (London: Epworth Press, 1931) , 4:102.
6. D. Michael Henderson, *John Wesley's Class Meetings: a Model for Making Disciples* (Nappanee, Ind.: Evangel Publishing House, 1997). 118-19
7. *Call to Action Steering Team Report*, 2010, p. 37.
8. "Pastor in the Present Tense: Your place and essential identity," Interview with Eugene Peterson, *Leadership Journal* (Summer 2011), www.christianitytoday.com/le/2011/summer/presenttense.html.
9. John Ortberg, "Redeeming Authority: Teaching with genuine authority spurs growth and awakens desire for God." *Leadership* (Summer, 2011), www.christianitytoday.com/le/2011/summer/redeemingauthority.html.

10. Richard J. Krejcer, "Statistics on Pastors," Frances A. Shaeffer Institute of Church Leadership Development in Anne Streaty Wimberly, "Pastor as Theologian: Nurturing Our Minds. *Circuit Rider* (Aug/Sept/Oct 2009) 21-23. Article is posted at www.circuitrider.com.

11. "Come Thou Fount of Every Blessing," *The United Methodist Hymnal* (Nashville, The United Methodist Publishing House,1989) 400

12. Jim C. Collins and Jerry I. Porras, *Built to Last* (New York: Harper Business, 1994), 43-45.

13. I strongly recommend *When Your Ministry Grows Past Your Leadership Style* by Bill Hybels, audio CD (South Barrington, Ill.: Willow Creek Association, 2004).

14. *Congregational Vitality: Towers Watson Report* from the *Call to Action Report*, June 2010, report p. 118. The complete Towers Watson research report can be found at www.umccalltoaction.org/the-challenge.

15. *Congregational Vitality: Towers Watson Report*, p. 91, slide 46.

16. *Congregational Vitality: Towers Watson Report*, p. 93, slide 48.

17. *Congregational Vitality: Towers Watson Report*, p. 98, slide 53.

2. Unleashing the Body of Christ

1. Steve Harper, *The Way to Heaven: The Gospel According to John Wesley* (Grand Rapids, Mich.: Zondervan, 1983, 2003), 121.

2. John Wesley, "The General Rules of The Methodist Church: The Nature, Design, and General Rules of Our United Societies," *The Book of Discipline of The United Methodist Church -2004. (Nashville: The United Methodist Publishing House, 2004).*

3. Wayne Cordeiro, *The Dream Releasers* (Regal Books, 2002.)

4. Walk to Emmaus, http://emmaus.upperroom.org/. The walk to Emmaus is an experience of Christian spiritual renewal and formation that begins with a three-day short course in Christianity. It is an opportunity to meet Jesus Christ in a new way as God's grace and love is revealed to you through other believers.

5. *Congregational Vitality: Towers Watson Report*, p. 79. slide 34.

6. *Congregational Vitality: Towers Watson Report*, p.79, slide 34.

7. *Congregational Vitality: Towers Watson Report*, p.80, slide 35.

8. *Congregational Vitality: Towers Watson Report*, p. 81, slide 36.

3. A People Made for Worship

1. *Wesley Hymnbook*, ed. Franz Hilderbrant (Kansas City: Lillenas Pub. Co., 1963) ix.

2. "Love Divine, All Loves Excelling," *The United Methodist Hymnal*, 384.

3. "A Charge to Keep I Have," *The United Methodist Hymnal*, 413.

4. John Wesley, *The Bicentennial Edition of the Works of John Wesley,* Volume 19, April 2, 1739 (Nashville: Abingdon Press, 1976–) See www.ministrymatters.com.

5. N.T. Wright, *Simply Christianity: Why Christianity Makes Sense* (Harper San Francisco, 2006), 3.

6. *Call to Action Steering Team Report*, p.35

7. *Congregational Vitality: Towers Watson Report*, p. 83, slide 38.

8. Faith Communities Today: http://faithcommunitiestoday.org/fact-2010 p.11
9. *Congregational Vitality: Towers Watson Report*, p.86, slide 41.

4. The Power of Small Groups
1. "We Are the Church," *The United Methodist Hymnal*, 558
2. D. Michael Henderson, *John Wesley Class Meetings* (Nappanee, Ind.: Evangel Publishing House, 1997), 145.
3. *Call to Action Steering Team Report*, p. 34.
4. *Call to Action Steering Team Report*, p. 35
5. *Congregational Vitality: Towers Watson Report*, p. 75, slide 30.
6. *Congregational Vitality: Towers Watson Report*, p.76, slide 31.
7. *Congregational Vitality: Towers Watson Report*, p.77, slide 32.

5. Reaching Across the Street and Around the World
1. Mother Teresa, "An Address at the National Prayer Breakfast" (February 3, 1994)
2. John Wesley, *The Works of John Wesley*, ed. Thomas Jackson (London: Wesley-Methodist Book Room, 1873) 8:310.
3. John Wesley, *The Works of John Wesley*, ed. Thomas Jackson, 8:47.
4. Harper, *The Way to Heaven,* 149.
5. John Wesley, *The Bicentennial Edition of The Works of John Wesley,* Volume 21, November 17, 1759.
6. John Wesley, *The Works of John Wesley,* ed. Thomas Jackson, February 7, 1776, 12:301.
7. D. Michael Henderson, *John Wesley's Class Meetings,* ed. Jackson, 125.
8. The following websites will offer more information about the programs listed.
Celebrate Recovery: http://www.celebraterecovery.com/
Stephen Ministry: http://www.stephenministries.org/
DivorceCare: http://www.divorcecare.org/
GriefShare; http://www.griefshare.org/
Financial Peace University: http://www.daveramsey.com/
Crown Ministries: http://www.crown.org/
Marriage Ministry: http://www.marriageministry.org/

Conclusion
John Wesley, "Thoughts upon Methodism," (pamplet) August 4, 1786

Appendix
1. *Call to Action Steering Team Report*, p.26.
2. *Congregational Vitality: Towers Watson Report*, p.111.
3. *Call to Action Steering Team Report*, p.23.